THE LIBRARY OF
AMERICAN
LIVES AND TIMES™

ELIZABETH CADY STANTON

Women's Suffrage and the First Vote

Dawn C. Adiletta

The Rosen Publishing Group's
PowerPlus Books™
New York

*With gratitude for all those women who have gone
before me, in obligation to those who will come after.
And with appreciation and love to JMA*

Published in 2005 by The Rosen Publishing Group, Inc.
29 East 21st Street, New York, NY 10010

First Edition

*Editor's Note: All quotations have been reproduced as they appeared in
the letters and diaries from which they were borrowed. No correction was
made to the inconsistent spelling that was common in that time period.*

Library of Congress Cataloging-in-Publication Data

Adiletta, Dawn C.
Elizabeth Cady Stanton : women's suffrage and the first vote / Dawn
C. Adiletta.
    v. cm. — (The library of American lives and times)
Includes bibliographical references and index.
Contents: Childhood and education — Finding a new role model —
Seneca Falls — Hurling thunderbolts and rocking babies — War, emanci-
pation, and betrayal — Stirring up women to rebellion — The history of
women's rights — The battle must finish with another generation.
ISBN 1-4042-2647-8 (lib. bdg.)
1. Stanton, Elizabeth Cady, 1815–1902—Juvenile literature. 2.
Feminists—United States—Biography—Juvenile literature. 3.
Suffragists—United States—Biography—Juvenile literature. 4.
Women's rights—United States—History—Juvenile literature. 5.
Women—Suffrage—United States—History—Juvenile literature. [1.
Stanton, Elizabeth Cady, 1815–1902. 2. Suffragists. 3. Women's rights.
4. Women—Suffrage. 5. Women—Biography.] I. Title. II. Series.

HQ1413.S67A64 2005
305.42'092—dc22
[B]
                                        2003019854

Manufactured in the United States of America

CONTENTS

Introduction

"My life has been one long struggle to do and say what I know to be right and true. I would not take back one brave word or deed. My only regret is that I have not been braver and truer in uttering the honest conviction of my own soul."

Elizabeth Cady Stanton in an 1860 letter
to her friend Amy Post

As a girl growing up in the early part of the nineteenth century, Elizabeth Cady Stanton enjoyed attending parties, playing games, and riding horses. She also had a passion for learning. As an adult, she continued to enjoy attending parties and playing games, as well as indulging in good food, but her passion had shifted. Stanton was focused on attaining rights for women, especially the right to vote.

Stanton was among the first Americans to equate being a citizen with having the right to vote. She based

Opposite: Elizabeth Cady Stanton, shown in an 1889 portrait by Anna E. Klumpke, said in an 1892 speech that personal responsibility and independence were vital to the happiness of all human beings. Rather than relying on another for help, "each soul must depend wholly on itself."

this connection on principles established during the American Revolution. When the U.S. Constitution became law in 1788, it promised that the government would rule only with the consent of the governed, by government leaders who were chosen through election. Yet women were not permitted to help choose their leaders. Although they paid taxes, women were not permitted to vote and they had no say in how those taxes would be spent. This was taxation without representation.

Stanton also sought reforms that guaranteed women pay that was equal to the pay earned by men for the same work. Equality for women, Stanton believed, should extend to opportunities in education and equal treatment under the law.

Elizabeth Cady Stanton's life was one long struggle to obtain civil rights. She died before she was able to vote legally in a national election. Stanton was successful, however, in expanding other legal rights and opportunities for women during her lifetime. This is the story of how a young girl from New York state grew up to be "America's Grand Old Woman."

1. Childhood and Education

Elizabeth Cady was born into a prosperous and influential family in Johnstown, New York, on November 12, 1815. Elizabeth, who was nicknamed Lizzie, was the eighth of eleven children born to Margaret Livingston Cady and Daniel Cady.

Margaret Livingston was almost 6 feet (1.8 m) tall, intelligent, and opinionated. Lizzie thought her mother looked like a queen. Margaret's friends described her as "refined and ladylike . . . with a cordial smile and a gentle sweet voice." Margaret Livingston came from a wealthy family with social and family ties to some of the most powerful people in New York. Lizzie's uncle, Peter Smith, was John Jacob Astor's partner in the fur trade. Astor was America's first millionaire.

Lizzie's father's beginnings were more humble. Daniel Cady grew up working on his family's farm in Canaan, New York. Daniel worked as a shoemaker for a short time. Shoemaking was not an exciting trade, but good workers could earn money quickly and many young shoemakers used their earnings to buy farms or to move to the West. Daniel Cady was forced to stop shoemaking after an accident left him blinded in one eye. He worked as a teacher for a while, and then he trained to become a lawyer.

There were no law schools when Daniel Cady was young. Instead, law students, who were called clerks, read law books, discussed cases, and helped to write legal papers for an established lawyer until the students were ready to take a bar exam, or state test. By 1799, Daniel Cady was a practicing attorney and his wealth and influence rapidly increased.

The Cady mansion in Johnstown, New York, shown in this mid-nineteenth-century photograph, reflected the family's wealth. The Cadys had about twelve servants on staff. These employees tended to the care of the house and grounds, the cooking, the children, and the laundry.

In 1801, when Daniel was twenty-eight and Margaret was sixteen, the couple married. Daniel invested in businesses, purchased land that he then rented to farmers, and entered politics. Daniel was elected to the state legislature in 1808. By the time Lizzie was born in 1815, he was a U.S. congressman. Daniel served in Congress for two years before returning to Johnstown, New York, as a judge. He was elected associate justice of the New York Supreme Court in 1847, a position he held until his retirement in 1855. Daniel was intellectual and stern. In spite of his being a politician, he did not enjoy public speaking and was often gruff to his friends and family.

The Cadys lived on the town square in one of Johnstown's largest houses. Johnstown is approximately 40 miles (64.4 km) northwest of Albany, the capital of New York. Because Johnstown was the county seat of Fulton County, it was a busy place in the 1800s. The county courts met there several times per year, bringing sheriffs, lawyers, clients, their friends and families, and the curious into town for trials. Lizzie and her sisters tagged along with the Cadys' servant Peter to listen to court cases.

There were always visitors to the Cady house. Politicians dropped by and clients came to seek Judge Cady's legal advice. Judge Cady also met with law clerks, young men whom the judge instructed in the law. Lizzie loved to listen to the conversations between her father and his clerks.

In addition to the everyday bustle around the house, there were also festive holidays and occasions, such as Christmas, Fourth of July, and general training day for the town's militia. Christmas was simple when Lizzie was a child. The Cadys did not put up a Christmas tree. They exchanged small presents, took gifts to poorer families, and ate a specially prepared meal. Lizzie later recalled that the Christmas stockings that hung by the kitchen hearth were filled with "a little paper of candy, one of raisins, another of nuts, a red apple, . . . and a bright silver quarter of a dollar in the toe."

The Fourth of July brought bonfires, fireworks, speeches, parades of soldiers, and booming cannons. The cannon shots and the passionate political speeches about the American Revolution frightened Lizzie, who later wrote, "No words can describe what I suffered with those explosions, great and small, and my fears lest King George . . . reappear [and] . . . burn our houses." The Revolution was not a distant event to Lizzie, as her grandfather James Livingston had been a colonel in the war. The patriotic speeches reminded Lizzie that, as an American citizen, she had rights that no one could take away from her.

General training days were the few days of the year in which men between the ages of sixteen and sixty practiced to be in the militia. Not everyone in town owned a gun or a rifle, so it was not unusual for some men to drill with brooms or rake handles. If the militia was well organized the marching and practicing were impressive to watch. If the troop was poorly organized, it was amusing. Many townspeople considered the day a holiday and brought picnic lunches to eat as they watched the show.

Despite the excitement of court sessions and holidays, Lizzie remembered Johnstown as a "gloomy-looking town." She thought her parents and nurses were too strict and recalled complaining to her nurse, "I am so tired of . . . no! no! no! At school, at home, everywhere it is no!"

Although Margaret and Daniel Cady had eleven children, five boys and six girls, most of the children died young. Four children died before Lizzie was born, and two more died before her thirteenth birthday. All of Lizzie's brothers died. Even though it was not unusual in the nineteenth century for children to die before they grew up, few families lost as many children as the Cadys did. The death of Lizzie's sister and brothers shadowed Lizzie's childhood in Johnstown. Later, when Elizabeth Cady Stanton looked back on her

Daniel Cady, shown in this portrait from around 1850, served in the legal profession for more than fifty years. He eventually became a judge of the New York State Supreme Court.

Margaret Livingston Cady, shown in a portrait from around 1840, was described by her daughter Elizabeth as being "courageous, self-reliant, and at her ease under all circumstances and in all places."

youth, she remembered her parents' grief and how, when the nearby church bells tolled for "funerals, church, or prayer meetings . . . Those clanging bells filled me with the utmost dread."

The death Lizzie remembered most vividly was that of her older brother Eleazer. In May 1826, Lizzie was ten and one-half. Twenty-year-old Eleazer, her father's favorite child, had just returned home after graduating from Union College. Unexpectedly, Eleazer became sick and died. Seeing her grieving father sit by her brother's coffin, Lizzie went to comfort him. "I wish you were a boy," Cady told his young daughter as she climbed into his lap.

Lizzie was strong and clever, which might have been why her father wished she were a boy. As a judge and lawyer, Daniel Cady knew that many traditions and laws would keep Lizzie from doing everything of which she was capable. No college would accept her as a student. No one would train her to be a lawyer, a minister, or a doctor.

Lizzie was hurt when her father said he wished she were a boy. Yet whenever her father's law students teased her about laws that treated women differently from men, Lizzie was not hurt, she was angry. If Lizzie were to marry, her money, her children, and even Lizzie herself, would become the property of her husband. Judge Cady and his students never thought to change the laws. As a child Lizzie wanted to cut the laws that were unfair to women out of her father's law books. Judge Cady laughed at Lizzie's suggestion and explained that books do not make laws, legislators do. Stanton later claimed that this was the start of her desire to make laws that treated everyone equally.

Hoping to ease her father's grief over Eleazer, Lizzie tried to " . . . be all my brother was . . . I decided to study Greek and learn to manage a horse." The Cadys' next-door neighbor, the Presbyterian minister Simon Hosack, gave her Greek lessons. Edward Bayard, a former class-mate of Eleazer's who married Lizzie's oldest sister, Tryphena, taught Lizzie how to play chess and to jump over fences on horseback.

Lizzie and her sisters began their elementary educa-tion at a local school where they learned the basics of reading and mathematics. The Cady girls were easy to recognize. Every year Margaret Cady dressed her three youngest daughters in matching red outfits. Not one of the girls liked it. "I still have a perfect vision of myself and sisters, as we stood up in the classes . . . all dressed alike in bright red flannel, black alpaca aprons, and, around the neck, a starched ruffle . . . We had red cloaks, red hoods, red mittens, and red stockings. For one's self to be all in red six months of the year was bad enough, but to have this costume multiplied by three was indeed monotonous . . . No words could do justice to my dislike of those red dresses."

When she was about eleven years old, Lizzie began studying at the Johnstown Academy. Girls and boys attended the same classes and played together at recess. Lizzie was among the academy's best students. When she won an award for her achievement in Greek, Lizzie proudly took it home to show her father. Her father congratulated her, kissed her on the forehead with affection, and sighed, "Ah, you should have been a boy!"

Lizzie wanted to attend Union College after she finished her classes at the academy, as her older brother Eleazer had done. Union College, however, refused to accept female students. Judge Cady told Lizzie that she did not need any additional education. He suggested that she learn how to "keep house and make puddings and pies" from her mother and her oldest sister, Tryphena. He also offered to let Lizzie rewrite his clerks' papers. Before the invention of typewriters, text for books and newspapers was first written by hand, and then typeset for printing. However, official records such as law cases were just neatly rewritten.

After graduating from Johnstown Academy in 1830, Lizzie spent six months learning housekeeping from her mother and older sister. She also learned how to present legal arguments as she copied Judge Cady's law clerks' papers. Her lessons in homemaking and lawmaking would both be useful to her in the future.

Edward Bayard finally convinced Judge Cady to let Lizzie travel 50 miles (80.5 km) from Johnstown to attend Emma Willard's Troy Female Seminary in Troy, New York. Lizzie, who had enjoyed competing with boys in the classroom, was displeased at the prospect of attending an all-female school. She feared the seminary would not challenge her mind. In 1831, fifteen-year-old Lizzie went

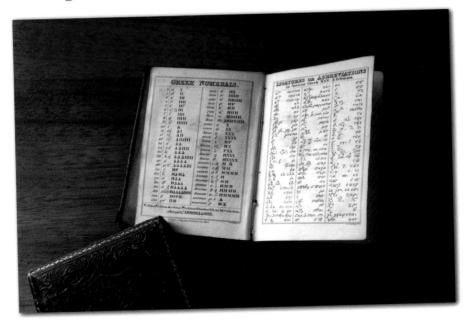

As a child, Elizabeth Cady Stanton owned this 1829 Greek lexicon. It was a vocabulary book designed to teach students Greek words they would encounter when reading the Greek New Testament bible.

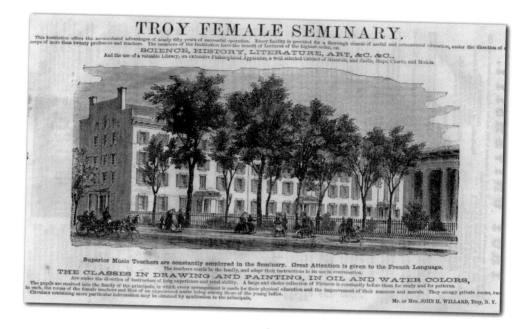

TROY FEMALE SEMINARY.

This Institution offers the accumulated advantages of nearly fifty years of successful operation. Every facility is provided for a thorough course of useful and ornamental education, under the direction of a corps of more than twenty professors and teachers. The members of the Institution have the benefit of Lectures of the highest order, on

SCIENCE, HISTORY, LITERATURE, ART, &C. &C.,

And the use of a valuable Library, an extensive Philosophical Apparatus, a well selected Cabinet of Minerals, and Shells, Maps, Charts, and Models.

Superior Music Teachers are constantly employed in the Seminary. Great Attention is given to the French Language. The teachers reside in the family, and adapt their instructions to its use in conversation.

THE CLASSES IN DRAWING AND PAINTING, IN OIL AND WATER COLORS,

Are under the direction of Instructors of long experience and tried ability. A large and choice collection of Pictures is constantly before them for study and for patterns. The pupils are received into the family of the principals, in which every arrangement is made for their physical education and the improvement of their manners and morals. They occupy private rooms, two in each, the rooms of the female teachers and that of an experienced nurse being among those of the young ladies. Circulars containing more particular information may be obtained by application to the principals,

Mr. or Mrs. JOHN H. WILLARD, Troy, N. Y.

The Troy Female Seminary, shown in a mid-nineteenth-century engraving, was the first school in the United States to instruct young women in higher education. The curriculum, or course of study, was similar to the material that young men studied at all-male colleges.

to Troy "in a hopeless frame of mind . . . [believing] I had already studied everything . . . . " Bayard, however, had known that the Troy Female Seminary was like a men's college when he had persuaded Judge Cady to send Lizzie to Troy. Judge Cady paid a substantial annual tuition of $300 for Lizzie to attend the school.

Lizzie took classes in algebra and geometry, logic, criticism and writing, literature, and modern history, as well as Greek, religion, and philosophy. "The novelty of everything made the new life more enjoyable than I had anticipated." Lizzie hated the food, however, and thought single-sex classes were silly.

Not all of Lizzie's education occurred in the classroom. Between 1800 and 1850, religious revivals swept through America. A similar heightened interest in religion had occurred during the middle of the 1700s. Christian ministers had called it a Great Awakening to God. The revivals of the 1800s were called the Second Great Awakening. Ministers traveled from town to town, preaching at large, outdoor revival meetings. Among the most famous ministers of the Second Great Awakening was Charles Finney. When Finney came to the town of Troy, Lizzie and other students attended his meetings. For someone like Lizzie, who was raised as a

Hugh Bridport's engraving from around 1829, based on a work by Alexander Rider, depicted a minister preaching at a camp meeting. During the Second Great Awakening, large outdoor revival meetings were often called camp meetings in some regions of the United States.

Presbyterian, Finney's meetings were amazing. Instead of strict sermons and somber prayers, there was music, shouting, and crying. Finney's faith was based on free will, the idea that people had a personal responsibility to decide whether or not to accept God's teachings.

This was a stunning concept to Lizzie who was raised to believe in the doctrine of predestination, or the belief that God had decided her fate before she was born and there was nothing she could do to change it. At first Lizzie was thrilled by Finney's message. Soon, however, the responsibility of guiding her soul toward salvation and away from hell frightened her and she became physically ill. Lizzie thought she was dying. She went home to Johnstown and then traveled with her father and Tryphena and Edward Bayard on a long trip to Niagara Falls in June 1831.

Lizzie felt better after talking to her family. Lizzie was willing to accept responsibility for her faith, but decided that Finney's religious style was too emotional for her. Although Stanton later claimed that Finney was a dangerous influence, his revival meetings began her lifelong questioning of religious authority and God.

In 1833, Lizzie's formal education ended after she graduated from the Troy Female Seminary at age seventeen. Her childhood was over, and she returned to her parents' home in Johnstown.

2. New Role Models

After graduating from the Troy Female Seminary, Elizabeth Cady spent the next six years behaving as many wealthy young women did. Because her parents' servants did most of the household chores, Elizabeth had time to attend parties, picnics, and dances. She rode horses, read books, wrote letters, and visited with friends and relatives. Nothing was more fun, though, than visiting her mother's wealthy cousin Gerrit Smith.

Gerrit Smith was a prominent abolitionist. Abolitionists, who wanted to abolish, or end, slavery immediately, were considered radicals. Although the antislavery movement became increasingly popular during the first half of the nineteenth century, many people shared the attitudes held by Judge Cady. The judge never

Gerrit Smith, photographed by Ezra Weld around 1850, was a social reformer. Smith was active in both the temperance and the abolitionist movements.

spoke in favor of slavery, but he refused to discuss the abolition of slavery and thought abolitionists were dangerous. Elizabeth's extended visits with Smith and his wife Ann in Peterboro, New York, gave her "a new inspiration in life and . . . new ideas of individual rights."

In October 1839, during one of those long visits, Elizabeth Cady met Henry B. Stanton, a tall, friendly young man. She was twenty-four. Henry was ten years older, an abolitionist, and a talented public speaker who could make "his audience both laugh and cry." Although Elizabeth had not yet formed her own opinion about slavery, she admired Henry's abolitionist beliefs, his speaking skills, and the way he was interested in what she had to say. Elizabeth was surprised when, soon after they met, Henry proposed marriage to her. She was not, however, too surprised to accept his offer.

Elizabeth's conservative family opposed her marriage to an abolitionist. Henry Stanton often encountered violence because of his ideas. Abolitionists were often justly accused of disregarding property laws. They ignored these laws because they did not believe human beings were property. Slave owners defended the practice of slavery by pointing out that the Bible does not condemn slavery. Abolitionists responded by saying that the Bible teaches people to treat others as they would wish to be treated themselves. Some abolitionists also hired women to speak against slavery in public. This broke with traditions that prohibited women from speaking to groups of men and women.

Mobs frequently threw stones and bottles at abolitionists, shouted at them when they tried to speak, and threatened to harm them. Henry Stanton claimed to have been mobbed by people in every state except Vermont, "where they abstained from that fascinating recreation."

The danger to abolitionists was real. The home of New York City abolitionist Lewis Tappan was burned in 1834. Illinois abolitionist and newspaper editor Elijah Lovejoy was killed by a mob in 1837.

If these were not reasons enough for Judge Cady, brother-in-law Edward Bayard, and cousin Gerrit

This 1840 broadside, created by R. S. Gilbert, used material that was first published after the December 4, 1833 Anti-Slavery Convention. The document was a manifesto, or a public declaration of beliefs or proposed action. The delegates to the 1833 convention announced their intention to form a national antislavery society.

Doctor Edward Bayard, shown in a photograph from the 1800s, was a lawyer before he chose to study to become a physician. He earned his medical degree from New York University in 1845.

Smith to worry about Henry Stanton as Elizabeth's future husband, there was also the issue of money. Abolitionists and antislavery agents received little pay.

Judge Cady knew that if Elizabeth married Henry Stanton any money she possessed became his to spend as he pleased. Elizabeth could end up a pauper. Edward Bayard reminded Elizabeth that married women lost what few legal rights they had as single women.

Husbands controlled their wives' inherited property. Married women could not keep money they earned, nor could they sign contracts, sue, borrow money, or establish credit. If a woman's husband died, she had the right to only one-third of his estate. The rest of the estate could be sold to pay off any existing debts. Women even needed their husband's approval to gain custody of their children. Nor was there any protection for wives or children against a husband's drunkenness or abuse. There were no grounds for divorce other than adultery.

Elizabeth knew all this. She had grown up listening to women weep over their misfortune in her father's law office. Judge Cady's law clerks had teased her with the realities of marriage laws.

Despite these warnings, Elizabeth was in love, and she wanted to marry Henry Stanton. However, after four months of constant pressure from so many members of her family, Elizabeth sadly broke off her engagement with Henry. The two agreed to keep corresponding.

Early in 1840, Henry Stanton was nominated to speak as a delegate to the first World Anti-Slavery Convention in London. After reading Henry's letter with news of his upcoming trip, Elizabeth realized that Henry would be gone for more than eight months. She decided to elope and hoped her family would come to accept her choice while she and Henry were in England.

Henry secretly returned to Johnstown, and, on May 1, 1840, the couple were married by a minister. Following Henry's suggestion, Elizabeth changed the traditional marriage vows. She promised to love and honor Henry, but she did not promise to obey him. The couple planned to live together as equals. There is no record that anyone from Elizabeth's family attended the wedding. The Stantons left town immediately after the service.

The honeymoon to England and the World Anti-Slavery Convention introduced Elizabeth Cady Stanton to abolitionists and reformers from both sides of the Atlantic Ocean. The men were interesting, but Elizabeth

The 1840 World Anti-Slavery Convention, which was held in London, England, was painted by Benjamin Robert Haydon in 1841. Henry Stanton can be seen in the first row. He is second from the right with long, thick sideburns. Although Henry made a speech in favor of including women at the convention, he probably voted against the idea.

was fascinated by the women, saying, "These were the first women I had ever met who believed in the equality of the sexes and who did not believe in the popular orthodox religion." The woman who impressed her the most was Lucretia Coffin Mott.

Lucretia Coffin Mott was born on Nantucket Island, Massachusetts, in 1793. Her parents were members of a religious Christian group known as Quakers, who raised their children to be active members of society. Mott had first been a teacher. Later she became a Quaker minister and a leader in the antislavery movement. Lucretia and her husband, James Mott, lived in Philadelphia, Pennsylvania.

Stanton saw Mott as "a broad, liberal thinker on politics, religion and all questions of reform, [who] opened . . . a new world of thought" to Stanton. Mott's ability to defend her position in an argument without appearing angry awed Stanton. Mott's skill at blending her work as an abolitionist with marriage and motherhood provided Stanton with her first role model.

Stanton was outraged when Mott and several other women delegates were refused the right to speak at the first World Anti-Slavery Convention because of their gender. As a result, Mott and Stanton resolved to "hold a convention as soon as we returned home, and form a society to advocate the rights of women."

The Stantons came back to the United States on December 24, 1840. To please his father-in-law and to earn a steady income, Henry Stanton gave up his job with the American Anti-Slavery Society to become a

Lucretia Coffin Mott, shown in an 1842 portrait by Joseph Kyle, delivered a sermon, in Britain, that Elizabeth Cady Stanton attended. Stanton had never heard a woman speak in public before.

lawyer. Elizabeth and Henry had their first child, Daniel, who was nicknamed Neil, on March 2, 1842. After studying with Judge Cady for about eighteen months in Johnstown, Henry accepted his first law job with a Boston company in October 1842.

At first the young family lived with Boston relatives, but after the birth of their second son, Henry Jr., in 1844, Judge Cady bought them a modern and fashionable house in Chelsea, located just outside of Boston. The Stantons quickly became part of the local intellectual community. Reformers and writers such as Lydia Maria Child, Stephen and Abby Kelley Foster, Frederick Douglass, John Greenleaf Whittier, Ralph Waldo Emerson, Nathaniel Hawthorne, and Maria Weston were frequent visitors at the Stanton home.

Elizabeth Cady Stanton enjoyed the challenge of being in charge of her house, the servants, and, by 1845, her three young sons: Daniel, Henry Jr., and Gerrit Smith Stanton. Yet Elizabeth still found time to attend temperance and antislavery lectures, musical performances, and literary discussion groups. She continued to correspond with Lucretia Mott, but their plans for a women's rights convention were put off for a time. Stanton also remained active in the politics of her home state of New York. Whenever she visited her parents in Albany, where Judge Cady had moved his family for several years, she collected signatures for petitions that supported the Married Woman's Property Act.

Property laws for married women were different in every state. Reformers focused on obtaining rights for married women such as ownership of and control over inherited property, earned wages, a legal voice in the care of their children, and protection for widows from being disinherited in their husbands' wills. When the New York Married Woman's Property Act passed in 1848, New York became the first state to allow married women to control their inherited property.

Elizabeth Cady Stanton was photographed with her son Henry Jr., who was nicknamed Kit, around 1854. Henry became a lawyer as an adult. For a time he ran a law practice with his father.

Although Elizabeth thrived in Boston, Henry was not doing as well as he hoped. He decided to move the family back to New York. In a letter from around 1847 to her cousin Libby Miller, Elizabeth wrote that she thought she could be happy in the country but that she was worried Henry would be bored. She was wrong.

3. Seneca Falls and Beyond

Henry Stanton hoped that his return to New York State in 1847 might improve his prospects for a political career. The family left the excitement of Boston for the small town of Seneca Falls.

Henry was quickly elected to the state senate. His political and antislavery work meant that he traveled often, leaving Elizabeth to manage the home and family without him. Their house, another gift from Judge Cady, was located outside the center of town and needed many repairs. Using money from her father, Elizabeth hired men to remodel, wallpaper, and paint the house. She still enjoyed being in charge, but "the novelty of housekeeping had passed away." Elizabeth had "poor servants, and an increasing number of children" and "so many cares . . . I suffered with mental hunger, which . . . is very depressing."

In the midst of this mental hunger came a July 1848 invitation from Jane Hunt, who lived in nearby Waterloo, New York. Hunt wrote that Elizabeth's old friend Lucretia Mott was in town. Hunt invited

Elizabeth Cady Stanton to her house for tea. Stanton readily accepted.

As Jane Hunt poured the tea, Stanton poured out her feelings of frustration and unhappiness. Lucretia Mott and Mott's sister, Martha Coffin Wright, and Hunt's neighbor Mary Ann McClintock were also at this party. The other women were older than Stanton was, and all of them except Stanton were Hicksite Quakers who believed that they should make the world a better place.

After listening to Stanton talk about the boredom of housework and the lack of educational and work

This daguerreotype of Seneca Falls, New York, was taken around 1855. The falls, which are part of the Seneca River, required ships to stop when they reached the rapids. In 1818, the Cayuga-Seneca Canal was built alongside the river so that ships could avoid the falls.

opportunities for women, the women decided to hold a convention, or a large public discussion that focused on one subject. Conventions were an effective way to encourage people to think and talk about new ideas. They usually lasted at least one or two days and followed an agenda, which helped to organize discussions by focusing the conversation on just one topic. The convention at Seneca Falls would be the first to discuss women's rights.

During the next few days the women arranged to use the Wesleyan Methodist Chapel in Seneca Falls as a meeting place. They put the following announcement in a local newspaper, the *Seneca County Courier*:

Woman's Rights Convention

A Convention to discuss the social, civil, and religious condition and rights of woman will be held in the Wesleyan Chapel, at Seneca Falls, N. Y., on Wednesday and Thursday, the 19th and 20th of July current; commencing at 10 o'clock A.M.

During the first day the meeting will be exclusively for women, who are earnestly invited to attend. The public generally are invited to be present on the second day, when Lucretia Mott, of Philadelphia, and other ladies and gentlemen, will address the convention.

The women also wrote a paper that outlined their grievances, or complaints, for convention attendees to discuss and then vote on to approve or disapprove. Stanton suggested they use the U.S. Declaration of Independence as a model to remind listeners that women were citizens, too. Stanton called their document the Declaration of Rights and Sentiments. This declaration listed sixteen grievances that included women being barred from college, married women losing control over their property, and, the most controversial complaint, women being prevented from using their franchise, or right to vote.

Yᵉ MAY SESSION OF Yᵉ WOMAN'S RIGHTS CONVENTION—Yᵉ ORATOR OF Yᵉ DAY DENOUNCING Yᵉ LORDS OF CREATION.

This cartoon, which appeared in the June 11, 1859, *Harper's Weekly*, is an early depiction of a women's rights convention. The artist chose to satirize, or to make fun of, this event.

Discussing women's voting rights seemed logical to Stanton. She had grown up hearing the expression "no taxation without representation." The patriotic Independence Day speeches of her childhood had taught her that Americans consented to be governed because they had a say in who would govern them. However, American women paid taxes without being able to vote for their leaders and representatives.

Lucretia Mott feared that listing the right to vote as a grievance was too daring. "Oh, Lizzie, thou will make us ridiculous!" she exclaimed. When Elizabeth discussed the

DECLARATION OF SENTIMENTS.

When, in the course of human events, it becomes necessary for one portion of the family of man to assume among the people of the earth a position different from that which they have hitherto occupied, but one to which the laws of nature and of nature's God entitle them, a decent respect to the opinions of mankind requires that they should declare the causes that impel them to such a course.

We hold these truths to be self-evident : that all men and women are created equal ; that they are endowed by their Cre-ator with certain inalienable rights, that among these are life, liberty, and the pursuit of happiness ; that to secure these rights governments are instituted, deriving their just powers from the consent of the governed. Whenever any form of government becomes destructive of these ends, it is the right of those who suffer from it to refuse allegiance to it, and to insist upon the institution of a new government, laying its foundation on such principles, and organizing its powers in such form as to them shall seem most likely to effect their safety and happiness.

The 1848 Declaration of [Rights and] Sentiments accused all men of depriving women of their natural rights. "He has compelled her to submit to laws, in the formation of which she had no voice." In the 1776 Declaration of Independence the "He" whom the patriots directed their grievances toward was Britain's King George.

plans for the convention with Henry Stanton, he thought the convention was a good idea. However, he believed that asking for the vote was so radical it would make the meeting seem laughable. When Elizabeth insisted on including women's franchise at the convention, Henry left town to avoid embarrassment.

Although Stanton and Mott worried that no one would attend the convention, a large crowd waited outside the chapel on July 19, 1848. Historical estimates of the number of attendees vary, but there may have been as many as three hundred people. Despite Stanton's prior arrangements, the chapel doors were locked. Stanton's young nephew was lifted through a window to open the building.

Since women had never been permitted to lead meetings, they had no experience in doing so. They asked Lucretia Mott's husband, James, to preside. When Stanton stood to read the Declaration of Rights and Sentiments she was nervous and her voice was timid. Her words, however, were bold. "We hold these truths to be self-evident: that all men and women are created equal . . . [man] has never permitted [woman] to exercise her inalienable right to the elective franchise." This was the first time that anyone had demanded the right to vote for women.

On July 20, men and women packed the chapel to discuss the declaration and to vote on the resolutions outlining women's rights. The resolution about women's right to vote caused the greatest debate. Stanton argued, "The right is ours," and continued, "The question now is, how shall we get possession of what rightly belongs to us . . . The great truth [is] that no just government can be formed without the consent of the governed . . . "

Finally, Frederick Douglass, an abolitionist, author, publisher, and former slave, persuaded the audience to accept the resolution calling for voting rights. Douglass argued "that the power to choose rulers" was the only right that would protect all other rights. The convention approved the resolution by an extremely close vote.

News of the Seneca Falls Convention quickly spread across the United States. A few newspapers were supportive. William Lloyd Garrison, the editor of the antislavery paper the *Liberator*, had voted to let women speak at the 1840 World Anti-Slavery Conference. Garrison cheered what he called the "Woman's Revolution." Horace Greeley, the editor of the New York *Tribune*, thought that asking for women's rights was a mistake, but he concluded his editorial by agreeing that Stanton's arguments were logical.

Most papers, however, made fun of the convention. "The women folks have just held a convention . . . and passed a sort of 'Bill of Rights' [asking] . . . to vote, to become teachers, legislators, lawyers, [ministers] . . . They should have resolved at the same time that [men] . . . wash dishes . . . handle the broom, darn stockings . . . look

Elizabeth Cady Stanton and Women's Rights

This illustration portrays Elizabeth Cady Stanton speaking at the 1848 Seneca Falls Convention. In her Seneca Falls address, Stanton prepared the audience for the long battle that lay ahead. To gain equal rights for women, Stanton said, the reformers would need to make their case again and again until they wore down their opponents.

This card was issued for the celebration held at Seneca Falls in 1908 and is added ...

Our Roll of Honor

Containing all the
Signatures to the "Declaration of Sentiments"
Set Forth by the First

Woman's Rights Convention,

held at
Seneca Falls, New York
July 19-20, 1848

LADIES:

Lucretia Mott	Sophronia Taylor	Rachel D. Bonnel
Harriet Cady Eaton	Cynthia Davis	Betsey Tewksbury
Margaret Pryor	Hannah Plant	Rhoda Palmer
Elizabeth Cady Stanton	Lucy Jones	Margaret Jenkins
Eunice Newton Foote	Sarah Whitney	Cynthia Fuller
Mary Ann M'Clintock	Mary H. Hallowell	Mary Martin
Margaret Schooley	Elizabeth Conklin	P. A. Culvert
Martha C. Wright	Sally Pitcher	Susan R. Doty
Jane C. Hunt	Mary Conklin	Rebecca Race
Amy Post	Susan Quinn	Sarah A. Mosher
Catherine F. Stebbins	Mary S. Mirror	Mary E. Vail
Mary Ann Frink	Phebe King	Lucy Spalding
Lydia Mount	Julia Ann Drake	Lovina Latham
Delia Mathews	Charlotte Woodward	Sarah Smith
Catherine C. Paine	Martha Underhill	Eliza Martin
Elizabeth W. M'Clintock	Dorothy Mathews	Maria E. Wilbur
Malvina Seymour	Eunice Barker	Elizabeth D. Smith
Phebe Mosher	Sarah R. Woods	Caroline Barker
Catherine Shaw	Lydia Gild	Ann Porter
Deborah Scott	Sarah Hoffman	Experience Gibbs
Sarah Hallowell	Elizabeth Leslie	Antoinette E. Segur
Mary M'Clintock	Martha Ridley	Hannah J. Latham
Mary Gilbert		Sarah Sisson

GENTLEMEN:

Richard P. Hunt	William S. Dell	Nathan J. Milliken
Samuel D. Tillman	James Mott	S. E. Woodworth
Justin Williams	William Burroughs	Edward F. Underhill
Elisha Foote	Robert Smallbridge	George W. Pryor
Frederick Douglass	Jacob Mathews	Joel Bunker
Henry W. Seymour	Charles L. Hoskins	Isaac VanTassel
Henry Seymour	Thomas M'Clintock	Thomas Dell
David Spalding	Saron Phillips	E. W. Capron
William G. Barker	Jacob P. Chamberlain	Stephen Shear
Elias J. Doty	Jonathan Metcalf	Henry Hatley
John Jones		Azaliah Schooley

This is a 1908 copy of the original list of people who signed the Declaration of Rights and Sentiments. Many of the signers withdrew their support later in response to negative public opinion.

beautiful and be . . . fascinating," quipped the editor of the *Lowell Massachusetts Courier*.

These published remarks did not bother Stanton. For even if they made fun of the convention, she explained in a letter to Mott, the publicity " . . . will start women thinking, and men, too . . . and when men and women think about a new question, the first step in progress is taken."

Women's rights conventions soon occurred in other New York communities and in the states of Massachusetts, Ohio, Pennsylvania, and Illinois. Stanton's life remained centered around her home and family in Seneca Falls, but steadily she increased her public activities and became a recognized promoter of women's rights.

Stanton was frequently asked to speak at women's rights conventions, including the first National Woman's

Rights Convention, which was held in Worcester, Massachusetts, in 1850. She usually declined the invitations because she did not want to leave her young children. Stanton did send agendas outlining discussion topics, as well as supportive letters to be read aloud when the conventions convened. She also wrote newspaper articles, including one for Amelia Bloomer's the *Lily*.

Amelia Bloomer was the postmistress for Seneca Falls and had attended the Seneca Falls Convention. The *Lily* began as a temperance paper that argued for people to avoid drinking alcohol. Stanton's regular contributions to the *Lily* broadened the newspaper's focus to include women's rights. Amelia Bloomer is most often remembered for her paper's promotion of the dress style that bears her name. Bloomers consisted of a knee-length skirt worn over long trousers. Reformers such as Stanton praised bloomers as a practical and comfortable fashion.

The more Stanton thought, wrote, and spoke on the topic of women's rights, the better she became at connecting those rights to other existing reform movements. For example, many people believed that temperance was good for the country. Therefore, Stanton included in her arguments the suggestion that women should be permitted to divorce alcoholic husbands. When she wrote about antislavery in America, Stanton said that no person, male or female, black or white, married or single, should be the legal property of another.

The February 1, 1855 edition of the *Lily* gave an opinion on a woman whose dowry, or bridal gift, became the property of her husband. Existing laws held that "a married woman in our State cannot possess a bridal gift!" Amelia Bloomer published the *Lily* twice per month and charged her readers fifty cents for a one-year subscription.

As Elizabeth's commitment to women's rights continued to grow, so did the size of her family. Elizabeth and Henry eventually had seven children. They had five boys and two girls. In order of their birth the children were Daniel Cady, Henry Brewster, Gerrit Smith, Theodore Weld, Margaret Livingston, Harriot Eaton, and Robert Livingston.

Elizabeth proudly raised a flag outside her house to announce each birth. A red flag went up for a boy. A white flag went up for a girl. Stanton recalled her own childhood as being filled with people who said "no, no, no" and was determined that her own children would have happier memories. She played games with them, built a gymnasium in her backyard, and never made them wake up early in the morning.

The three oldest boys were frequently in trouble. Stanton called them her "young savages." They jumped off roofs, threw rocks at people's houses, smoked cigars, and cussed. Once they put their baby brother Theodore on top of the chimney. Another time they tested a homemade life preserver made of corks on Theodore. The child was tied to the life preserver and then placed into the river to see if he would float. Although there were a few broken bones, and some close calls, no one was seriously hurt. Stanton was always afraid, however, that if she was not there, things would become even more out of control.

For a while Stanton home-schooled her children, but she stopped as the babies kept coming and the boys kept causing trouble. On one of Henry's infrequent visits

Currier & Ives 1851 lithograph depicts a woman wearing a bloomer costume. To add to the newfound freedom that came from wearing bloomers, some suffragists cut their long hair into a shorter bob.

Nineteenth-century female fashions often caused health and safety issues for women. Tight corsets crushed internal organs and made it difficult for women to breathe. Long, heavy skirts and petticoats were easy to trip on, especially when climbing stairs.

In January 1851, Elizabeth Cady Stanton's cousin and friend, Elizabeth Smith Miller, visited Seneca Falls wearing a gathered knee-length skirt over full ankle-length trousers. Stanton and other reformers, such as Susan B. Anthony and Lucy Stone, admired the outfit and adopted the "Reform Dress," as they called it. The look became associated with women's rights.

After Amelia Bloomer printed a sketch of the Reform Dress in the June 1852 issue of the Lily, people began to call the short skirts "Bloomer's dress" or "Bloomers" for the Lily's editor. Many people thought bloomers looked silly or indecent. Henry Stanton had no objection to the style, although he teased Elizabeth about showing her legs. Judge Cady and the Stanton's older sons, however, begged Elizabeth not to wear bloomers in public.

Later, in response to public criticism, many women wondered if they were spending too much time talking about their clothes instead of women's rights. Reluctantly they gave up their short skirts.

home, Henry and Elizabeth made the decision to send the older boys to boarding school.

Although Stanton's reluctance to leave her children kept her in Seneca Falls, her many visitors kept her intellectually involved in political events. The Stanton household frequently provided hospitality to reformers who had come to Seneca Falls to lecture. Henry understood how much Elizabeth enjoyed being politically informed and so he regularly sent her political updates from the state capital in Albany and from Washington, D.C.

Houseguests and visitors found the Stantons charming, but not everyone in Seneca Falls shared the same opinion. Elizabeth Cady Stanton's willingness to attract attention, whether by wearing bloomers, visiting Irish shanties, or raising a flag with the birth of each child, made Elizabeth the topic of local gossip. During one of Elizabeth's infrequent trips away from Seneca Falls, Amelia Bloomer teased Stanton that she should hurry home: "People have nothing to talk about while you are gone."

4. Hurling Thunderbolts and Rocking Babies

Elizabeth Cady Stanton first met Susan Brownell Anthony in the spring of 1851. These two women would form a powerful partnership for women's rights that would last more than fifty years.

Susan Brownell Anthony was born on February 15, 1820. She was raised near Adams, Massachusetts, as a Hicksite Quaker. When Susan was seventeen, a nationwide economic depression called the Panic of 1837 caused many businesses to fail, including her father's cotton mill. Susan became a teacher to help support her family. In 1845, hoping for a fresh start, the Anthonys moved to Rochester, New York, and took up farming.

Susan B. Anthony continued teaching in New York and became headmistress of the female department of the Canajoharie Academy. By 1849, Susan had grown weary of teaching and wanted to devote more time toward social reform. When her father opened an insurance company, she quit her job to manage the family farm and joined the local temperance association and antislavery society. As the debate over slavery heightened in the

1840s and 1850s, the Anthonys' farm became part of the Underground Railroad, a secret network of hiding places for fugitive slaves escaping to Canada and freedom.

Susan's activism in the antislavery movement took her to Seneca Falls in the spring of 1851 to hear William Lloyd Garrison speak. She stayed with her friend Amelia Bloomer. Bloomer introduced her to Garrison and to Elizabeth Cady Stanton.

Stanton later wrote, "How well I remember the day! . . . William Lloyd Garrison having announced an anti-slavery meeting in Seneca Falls, Miss Anthony came to attend it . . . . [He] was my guest. Walking home after the adjournment we met Mrs. Bloomer and Miss Anthony on the corner of the street, waiting to greet us. There she stood, with her good earnest face and genial smile . . . the perfection of neatness and sobriety. I liked her thoroughly. . . ."

Elizabeth Cady Stanton and Susan B. Anthony exchanged letters for a time. Their shared passion for

Napoleon Sarony photographed Susan B. Anthony around 1870. Anthony believed that coeducational colleges, or schools that students of both sexes attend, would serve to educate woman far better than single-sex schools had.

social reform soon brought Anthony frequently to Seneca Falls and to Stanton's home.

The two women quickly discovered the best method for working together. Stanton found it difficult to leave her boisterous children unattended. Anthony, a single woman with fewer domestic obligations, was not good at writing speeches. Anthony gathered data from newspapers and law books and brought suitcases filled with her research to Seneca Falls. Then, while Anthony oversaw the house and the children, Stanton used the research to write newspaper articles, convention letters, and speeches for Anthony to present in public. Anthony became the voice for Stanton's written words. The two were to become inseparable in the public mind. Stanton wrote, " . . . Our speeches may be considered the united product of our two brains . . . I forged the thunderbolts," she said, "[Susan] fired them."

In January 1852, Anthony was angered when the chairman of the Sons of Temperance convention in Albany, New York, told her that, although women were invited to "listen and learn" at the convention, they were not to speak. In response, Anthony helped to form the Woman's State Temperance Society in Rochester, New York, that same year. She asked her friend Stanton to write and deliver the opening speech. In her address Stanton proclaimed that a woman who was married to an alcoholic had adequate cause to seek a divorce. The attendees to the association then elected

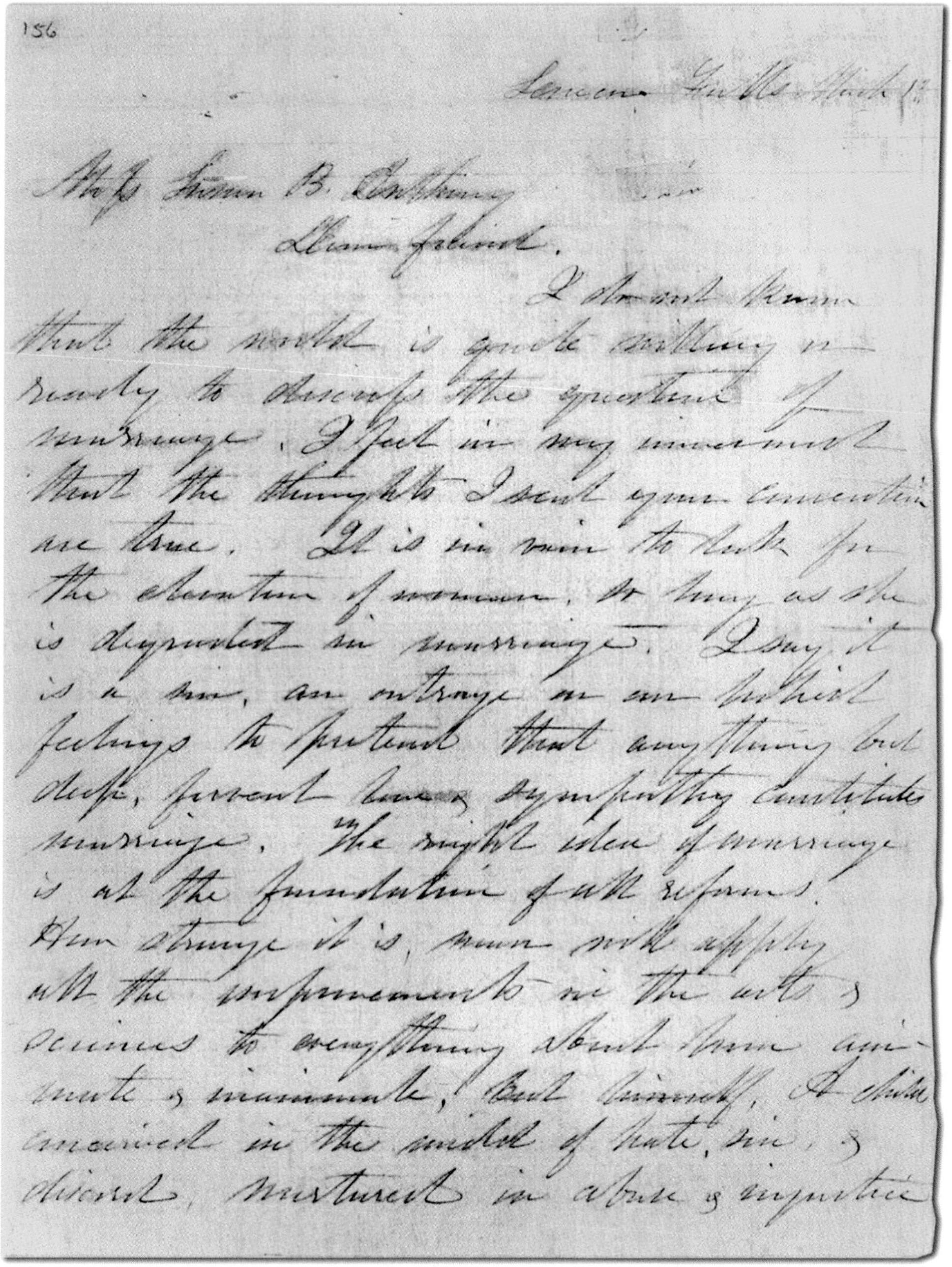

156

Seneca Falls March 1st

Miss Susan B. Anthony

Dear friend,

I do not know that the world is quite willing or ready to discuss the question of marriage. I feel in my innermost that the thoughts I sent your convention are true. It is in vain to look for the elevation of woman, so long as she is degraded in marriage. I say it is a sin, an outrage on our holiest feelings to pretend that anything but deep, fervent love & sympathy constitutes marriage. The right idea of marriage is at the foundation of all reforms. How strange it is, man will apply all the improvements in the arts & sciences to everything about him animate & inanimate, but himself. A child conceived in the midst of hate, sin, & discord, nurtured in abuse & injustice

Elizabeth Cady Stanton composed this letter for Susan B. Anthony on March 1, 1852. Stanton wrote that if women were to advance in society through social reforms, then the rights of married women would need to be addressed at the same time. The two were intertwined.

The Confirmed Drunkard, published around 1826, is one in a series of four engravings by J. W. Barber that depict the destructive effects of alcohol abuse on the drinker and his family.

Stanton president and Anthony secretary.

Stanton soon began to expand the work of the temperance association to include women's rights. In addition to advocating divorce law reform so that women could divorce alcoholic husbands, she sought property law reforms so that drunken husbands could not sell the family home to pay off their debts. Stanton also believed that churches and missionaries should work to end poverty in America, rather than going abroad to convert "the heathen across the ocean. . . ." In a speech Stanton delivered on April 20, 1852, she said, "Let us feed and clothe the hungry and the naked, gather children into schools, and provide reading-rooms and decent homes for young men and women thrown alone upon the world . . . [This] would do much more to prevent immorality and crime in our cities than all the churches in the land could ever possibly do . . . ."

Stanton's strong views offended some members of the association. The more conservative women in the group voted to allow men into the group. One year later, the association voted to grant men a vote and then subsequently voted Stanton out from her position as president. Surprised and angry, Anthony quit the organization she had helped to create. The outcome did not bother Stanton and she consoled Anthony by writing, "We have other and bigger fish to fry."

Society was often opposed to allowing women to speak in public or to granting women their civil rights, because these advances went against the custom of separate spheres for men and women. Some people believed that only men belonged in the public sphere of business and government. These people thought women should stay in the domestic sphere and tend to children and homemaking. Stanton thought each individual should choose his or her own sphere. She wrote in 1848, "Man has quite enough to do to find out his own individual calling, without . . . [trying] to find out also where every woman belongs . . . Every man has a different sphere, in which he may or may not shine, and it is the same with every woman . . . ."

After having four sons, Stanton finally gave birth to a daughter in October 1852, whom she named Margaret for her mother. Stanton wanted her daughter to have

ADDRESS

TO THE

Legislature of New-York,

ADOPTED BY THE

STATE WOMAN'S RIGHTS CONVENTION,

HELD AT ALBANY,

Tuesday and Wednesday, February 14 and 15, 1854.

PREPARED BY

ELIZABETH CADY STANTON,

Of Seneca Falls, N. Y

ALBANY:
WEED, PARSONS AND COMPANY.
1854.

This is the title page to Stanton's February 1854 address to the New York legislature in Albany on behalf of women's rights. Fifty thousand copies of this speech were printed. Stanton took three of her children with her to Albany. The children stayed in a hotel with the Stantons' housekeeper while their mother delivered her speech.

the opportunities that she had been denied and thereafter Stanton increased her activism in women's rights.

Stanton agreed to testify on women's rights before the New York Senate in 1854. Anthony helped Stanton to prepare her presentation. When Judge Cady read about Stanton's upcoming testimony in the newspaper, he demanded to see her. Much later Stanton claimed that her father had liked her speech and had helped her to revise it before it was delivered. Stanton's letters written at the time, however, reveal that her father was so angry about the upcoming event that he threatened to disinherit her if she spoke. Henry was unhappy, as well. As a state senator, he should have been present in the legislature when his wife testified on February 14, 1854, but he was not.

Stanton's demands included allowing widows to inherit their husbands' estates, allowing mothers to become guardians of their children, permitting wives to divorce abusive husbands, and permitting all women to collect wages, to make contracts in their own names, to sit on juries, and, of course, to vote. Newspapers praised Stanton's speech for its logic and persuasiveness. The legislature, however, refused to grant women any additional rights.

Both Judge Cady and Henry Stanton were embarrassed by Elizabeth's advance into the public sphere. Stanton wrote to Anthony in September 1855, "I passed through a terrible scourging when last at my father's. . . .

To think that all in me of which my father would have felt a proper pride had I been a man is deeply mortifying to him because I am a woman . . . Henry sides with my friends who oppose me in all that is dearest to my heart. They are not willing that I would write even on the woman question. But I will both write and speak."

As Stanton struggled to combine being the mother of young children with doing the reform work that interested her, her reliance on Anthony continued. Anthony, who remained single and self-supporting, was angry whenever Stanton announced the birth of another child or when other feminists married. Anthony knew these women would expect her to do the work they could no longer do. Stanton asked Anthony to be understanding: "My whole soul is in the work, but my hands belong to my family."

The birth of Stanton's seventh and last child, Robert, in March 1859, left Stanton weak and depressed. She wanted to travel as Henry did and to join Anthony in speaking engagements concerning women's rights. She had written to Anthony in 1856, "I pace up and down . . . like a caged lion, longing to bring nursing and housekeeping cares to a close. I have other work at hand."

In October 1859, the abolitionist John Brown, a friend of Elizabeth's cousin Gerrit Smith's, led an attack on the federal arsenal at Harpers Ferry, Virginia. Brown hoped to seize arms from the warehouse for a rebellion of enslaved African Americans. Brown was arrested, tried, convicted of treason, and then executed in December.

Stanton (*left*) and Anthony (*right*) wrote to each other often. In a June 1856 letter, Stanton asked Anthony to respect that some suffragists, or individuals who fought for the right to vote, required time to be with their family: "It is not well to be in the excitement of public life all the time . . . You need rest too, Susan. Let the world alone awhile. We cannot bring about a moral revolution in a day or year." Napoleon Sarony photographed Stanton and Anthony around 1870.

Gerrit Smith, who feared his own arrest because he had helped to fund the raid, committed himself to a mental institution. That same month on October 31, Judge Cady died, crushing Elizabeth's hopes of ever winning her father's approval. His will left her an inheritance of approximately $50,000.

Susan B. Anthony recognized her friend's distress and came to Seneca Falls at Christmas. Anthony gave Stanton a job. She needed another women's rights speech and she wanted Stanton to present it.

Stanton returned to Albany to speak before the New York legislature a second time on March 19, 1860.

Augustus Köllner's watercolor of Albany, New York, from around 1845, depicts the city on the horizon, set alongside the banks of the Hudson River. The two domed buildings in the skyline of New York State's capital are City Hall (*left*) and the State Building (*right*).

Stanton and Anthony argued that married women should have all the legal rights of American citizens, not the legal standing of slaves. Calling her speech "A Slave's Appeal," Stanton compared the legal power of husbands with that of a slave's master. A wife's work and wages belonged to her husband. He controlled where she lived, what would happen to her children, even her own fate. Guessing that the legislators would claim that women were safe in their sphere, Stanton pointed out that women were sometimes the mothers, sisters, and wives of dishonest, alcoholic, and abusive men. There was nothing a woman could encounter in the world that she could not also confront in her own home. Only the vote could truly protect women by enabling them to vote for the laws and leaders that would govern them.

Although the legislature refused to consider granting women the vote, the day after Stanton's speech the legislators voted in favor of expanding the rights of married women. Widows were permitted to manage their husbands' estates and mothers were allowed to be the guardians of their own children.

5. War, Emancipation, and Betrayal

Judge Cady's death freed Elizabeth Cady Stanton to be even bolder in her actions. Although she was saddened by her father's death, she could no longer make him angry. Her inheritance reduced the Stantons' financial worries. Inspired by her success in Albany, Elizabeth Cady Stanton accepted more public appearances. She was aided in this endeavor by Margaret Cady, who happily invited her grandchildren to Johnstown for school breaks and summer vacations.

In May 1860, Stanton traveled to New York City and spoke at the American Anti-Slavery Society, where she demanded the vote for both white and black women. The 1860 Tenth National Woman's Rights Convention was meeting in New York City at the same time, and Stanton attended that convention as well. Although Stanton's letters had been read aloud at every National Convention since 1850, this was her first personal appearance. She made a dramatic presentation on behalf of divorce. Most nineteenth-century people thought divorce was shameful and believed couples should stay married regardless of the circumstances. The audience was shocked by Stanton's remarks. Lucy Stone, one of the leaders of the convention, objected to Stanton's speech.

Lucy Stone was one of the first American women to attend college. After graduating in 1847 from Oberlin College in Ohio, Stone became a professional lecturer for the New England Anti-Slavery Society. In 1850, only two years after the Seneca Falls Convention, Stone helped to organize a National Woman's Rights Convention in Worcester, Massachusetts. This was the first of the annual national women's conventions. Lucy Stone was far more conservative than Stanton despite being among the last to give up wearing bloomers and keeping her own name after she married the abolitionist Henry Blackwell.

The objections Stanton encountered the following year in January 1861 were more dangerous. Abraham Lincoln's election as U.S. president in November 1860 had angered many

Lucy Stone, shown in a daguerreotype from around 1850, saved her earnings for nine years to attend Oberlin College. Stone, who was considered a fine speaker, organized a female debating club at Oberlin. To persuade others of the need for reform, Stone urged women to learn how to pose questions and construct arguments.

Southerners who thought that he would end the institution of slavery. Lincoln's election annoyed many abolitionists who feared that he would not end it soon enough. Stanton joined a group of abolitionists touring northern New York and delivered some of her strongest antislavery speeches. Angry crowds shouted at the abolitionists, hung Anthony in effigy, and threatened violence. Henry Stanton had seen mobs such as these when he was an antislavery speaker in the 1830s. He was worried and wrote to Elizabeth on January 12, "I think you risk your lives . . . [they] would as soon kill you as not." Elizabeth heeded his advice and returned home. Later, around February 1861, she rejoined the group once they reached Albany.

The Stantons left Seneca Falls permanently in the spring of 1862, when Henry became the deputy commissioner of the U.S. Customs House in New York City. Delighted, Elizabeth moved her family into a Manhattan townhouse that included a room for Susan B. Anthony.

In addition to writing as a journalist, Henry B. Stanton, shown in a photograph, wrote two books, the 1849 *Sketches of Reforms and Reformers in Great Britain and Ireland* and the 1887 *Random Recollections*.

The family arrived in the city as the first year of the Civil War was ending and the first antidraft riots began. Even in the North, not everyone supported the Civil War. Some Northerners felt the Southern states should be allowed to leave the Union. Other Northerners opposed a draft that required them to go into battle. In July 1863, an angry mob battled both soldiers and police officers outside the Stantons' front door. Elizabeth confided to her friends in a letter that she feared, as "Henry, Susan and I were so identified with reform and reformers, we might at any moment be subjects of vengeance." Elizabeth retreated with the children to Johnstown until the situation calmed down.

Henry Stanton believed he was the victim of revenge of a different sort in 1863. His job at the Customs House required that he collect bonds from shippers, which were paid in advance, to prevent anything from being smuggled to the South. Once shipments arrived in the correct port, the bonds were returned to the shipper. If the shipments did not arrive at the right destination, the bonds became the property of the government. The Stantons' oldest son, Daniel, who worked with his father, accepted a bribe to forge his father's name on paperwork in order to return bonds to the shipper early.

Next Spread: This engraving of protesters attacking a brownstone during the New York City antidraft riots appeared in the July 25, 1863 *New York Illustrated News*. Working-class whites targeted blacks during the five days of rioting. Many white workers feared that the newly emancipated slaves would move to the North and compete with whites for jobs.

When it was discovered that bonds were missing, Henry was accused of stealing them. Daniel finally confessed to his father what he had done. Henry quietly fired his son and accepted responsibility as Daniel's father and boss. Henry was forced to resign in December 1863. Both Henry and Elizabeth believed that Henry's political enemies had tricked Daniel. Neither parent wanted to blame their son.

Henry was unemployed for one year. Eventually he returned to one of the jobs he had held before accepting the position at the Customs House. He found employment as a writer for the New York *Tribune*.

As the Civil War took men of all ages to the battlefields, women increased their work on farms and factories by planting and harvesting crops to feed armies, or by making uniforms, shoes, guns, and ammunition to equip soldiers. A few women dressed as men and went to war. Some women, such as Clara Barton, volunteered as nurses and dodged bullets during battles as they tended the wounded. Others volunteered to collect clothing and cloth to make bandages. During the war Stanton and Anthony increased their antislavery work.

Stanton and Anthony agreed on the need for total emancipation of enslaved African Americans, but felt differently about the war and its impact on society. Stanton supported the war and was pleased when her son Henry Jr. enlisted. Anthony, a Quaker pacifist, opposed the war and feared that the war was being fought only to preserve

Through the weary years of the war Clara Barton stayed at her post.

This early-twentieth-century engraving by William M. Allison depicts Clara Barton, a Civil War nurse and founder of the American Red Cross, tending to a wounded soldier. In addition to providing assistance on the battlefield, the Red Cross also aids citizens during periods of hardship caused by natural disasters such as tornadoes, droughts, and floods.

the union of states and was not being fought to end slavery. Stanton, who worked for Lincoln's Republican Party, trusted that the end of slavery would bring all citizens, regardless of their race or gender, equality and the vote.

Anthony worried that the war distracted people from women's rights and that conservative New York politicians, who were then in power, would undo some of the progress women had made. She was right. The annual National Woman's Rights conventions temporarily stopped meeting once the war began. Republican officials had suggested that the nation needed to focus on the war. In 1862, the New York legislature removed some of the married women's property rights previously granted in 1860, and again it denied mothers an equal voice in their children's guardianship and prohibited widows from managing their husbands' estates. Without the vote, women's rights were not secure.

President Lincoln moved slowly toward abolition. He had been president for nearly two years before the Emancipation Proclamation was announced in January 1863. Furthermore, the Emancipation Proclamation ended slavery only in the rebelling states in order to keep those slave states that had not seceded in the Union. In response Stanton and Anthony formed the National Woman's Loyal League. This group organized the country's largest petition drive in support of the Thirteenth Amendment to the U.S. Constitution, which would end slavery throughout the United States.

The U.S. Constitution and its amendments, or the additions or changes to the Constitution, define how the U.S. government is to function and what rights are guaranteed to U.S. citizens. To pass an amendment, both the House of Representatives and the Senate must vote in favor of the proposed amendment. Next, three-quarters of the U.S. states must agree to an amendment in order to ratify the amendment, or make it the law. The first ten amendments, called the Bill of Rights, were ratified in 1791.

The first thirteen amendments refer to "citizens." In theory, these amendments therefore grant all adult citizens the same rights. The Fourteenth Amendment, however, added the word "male" to the Constitution, qualifying that the right to vote could not be "denied to any of the male inhabitants" who were twenty-one years old and U.S. citizens. The Fifteenth Amendment declared "the right to vote shall not be denied on account of race, color or previous condition of servitude." Gender was left out. The Fourteenth Amendment and the Fifteenth Amendment made it harder for women to secure the right to vote.

Thirty-Eighth **Congress of the United States of America;**

At the *second* Session,

Begun and held at the City of Washington, on Monday, the *fifth* day of December, one thousand eight hundred and sixty-*four*

A RESOLUTION

Submitting to the legislatures of the several States a proposition to amend the Constitution of the United States

Resolved by the Senate and House of Representatives of the United States of America in Congress assembled,

(two-thirds of both Houses concurring) that the following article be proposed to the legislatures of the several States as an amendment to the constitution of the United States; which, when ratified by three-fourths of said legislatures, shall be valid, to all intents and purposes, as a part of the said constitution, namely: Article XIII. Section 1. Neither slavery nor involuntary servitude, except as a punishment for crime whereof the party shall have been duly convicted, shall exist within the United States, or any place subject to their jurisdiction. Section 2. Congress shall have power to enforce this article by appropriate legislation.

Schuyler Colfax
Speaker of the House of Representatives.

H. Hamlin
Vice President of the United States and President of the Senate

Approved February 1, 1865.   *Abraham Lincoln*

PRIVATE LAWS

This is the March 2, 1861 joint resolution proposing that Congress had no authority to amend the U.S. Constitution to interfere with slavery in the states. A joint resolution means that both the Senate and the House of Representatives voted in favor of a proposed bill. However, the states failed to ratify this 1861 amendment.

With the help of women, the Thirteenth Amendment was ratified in June 1865 after the end of the war. Slavery in the United States was over.

However, as abolitionists and women's rights supporters knew, only the vote protected freedom. Stanton was joyous when a Fourteenth Amendment expanding the franchise was written by abolitionists and Republicans in 1865. Nearly twenty years after the Seneca Falls Convention, she believed that finally there would be universal suffrage.

The drafted amendment granted only African American men the right to vote. Stanton was stunned. She believed that complete justice required giving women those same rights of citizenship. The two causes were united in her mind. Never had it occurred to her that abolitionists could think otherwise. Frederick Douglass had supported giving women the vote in Seneca Falls. Wendell Phillips had sided with women at the 1840 World Anti-Slavery Convention. Phillips, the president of the Anti-Slavery Society, called the Fourteenth Amendment "the Negro's hour" and explained to Stanton that women's suffrage might hurt the chance of African Americans obtaining the vote. Stanton retorted to Phillips in a May 1865 letter, "Do you believe the African race is composed entirely of males?"

Stanton and Anthony felt betrayed by the American Anti-Slavery Society and the Republican Party. The

Fourteenth Amendment implied that only males were citizens and the Fifteenth Amendment prohibited states from denying the right to vote based on "race, color, or previous condition of servitude" without providing women similar protections. Stanton and Anthony lobbied against these amendments.

Most abolitionists and suffragists agreed that black men should receive the vote before black or white women. Sojourner Truth, a female former slave and a traveling minister who gave powerful antislavery speeches, believed that women's suffrage and black suffrage should be granted at the same time.

When white suffragists accused Stanton of racism because she fought against the Fourteenth Amendment, Sojourner Truth stayed at the Stantons' home and sat by Elizabeth's side at the National Woman Suffrage Association meetings.

Stanton and Anthony's attacks on the amendments did sound racist, especially to abolitionists. Stanton and Anthony argued that uneducated black men and immigrants should not be allowed to vote while educated white women could not. In their efforts to stop the amendments from being ratified, or passed into law, Stanton and Anthony joined forces with George Train. Train was a wealthy traveling salesman and actor. He was also a racist who believed that African Americans should be denied the vote. One of the reasons Stanton and Anthony were willing to appear in public with

Train was because he provided financial backing for their women's rights newspaper, the *Revolution*.

Stanton and Anthony had wanted to start a women's rights newspaper for some time. The *Revolution*'s motto was "Principle, Not Policy: Justice, Not Favors.—Men, Their Rights And Nothing More: Women, Their Rights And Nothing Less." The paper was first published in January 1868 and it provided Stanton with an outlet in which to publish her radical editorials and speeches in support of women's rights. Stanton was the journal's senior editor and primary author. Anthony managed the

Alfred Waud's engraving depicts African American citizens casting their ballots at the polls. This engraving appeared in the November 16, 1867 edition of *Harper's Weekly*, but the Fifteenth Amendment to the U.S. Constitution, which granted African American males the right to vote, was not ratified until March 30, 1870.

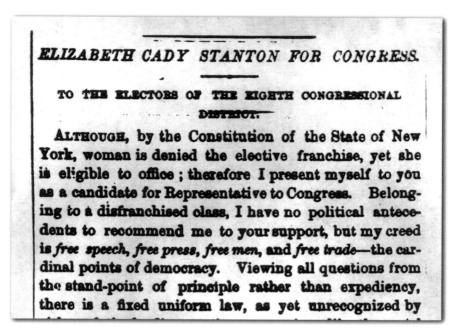

ELIZABETH CADY STANTON FOR CONGRESS.

TO THE ELECTORS OF THE EIGHTH CONGRESSIONAL DISTRICT.

ALTHOUGH, by the Constitution of the State of New York, woman is denied the elective franchise, yet she is eligible to office ; therefore I present myself to you as a candidate for Representative to Congress. Belonging to a disfranchised class, I have no political antecedents to recommend me to your support, but my creed is *free speech, free press, free men,* and *free trade*—the cardinal points of democracy. Viewing all questions from the stand-point of principle rather than expediency, there is a fixed uniform law, as yet unrecognized by

In the October 13, 1866 *National Anti-Slavery Standard* Elizabeth Cady Stanton announced that she was running for the U.S. Congress in New York State. Although she did not win the election, Stanton was pleased that twenty-four "unknown friends" had voted for her.

office and paid the *Revolution*'s bills. Stanton tackled difficult subjects, many of which concerned the abuse of women and children. Her writing disturbed many of her contemporaries.

The publication of the *Revolution* and their relationship with Train divided Stanton and Anthony from most of the Republican Party, other abolitionists, and other supporters of women's suffrage. After almost two and one-half years of publishing their paper, the women were forced to sell the paper when Train, who was then in Europe, withdrew his financial support.

6. Stirring Up Women to Rebellion

Henry Stanton's Custom House scandal, the fights over the amendments, and the split with other reformers made living in New York City less attractive to Elizabeth Cady Stanton. In 1868, she purchased a home in the small town of Tenafly, New Jersey. The house was near a railroad station, which made it easy for Henry to travel back and forth to Manhattan and to his job at the New York *Tribune*. Nevertheless, Henry and Elizabeth began spending less time together.

Although they never legally separated or divorced and the couple continued to see each other, Henry maintained a home in New York City while Elizabeth's primary residence was in Tenafly. By this time, the Stanton children were all either in college or attending boarding school. During the summers and holidays the children spent time visiting with both parents.

In May 1869, after bitter disagreements over the Fifteenth Amendment and accusations that Stanton's opinions were too radical, the women's rights movement divided into two groups. Elizabeth Cady Stanton,

This was Elizabeth Cady Stanton's home on Highwood Avenue in Tenafly, New Jersey. Elizabeth placed mosquito netting around the veranda, or covered porch, so that during the summer evenings Henry could sit outside and smoke "his pipe, could muse and gaze at the stars unmolested."

Susan B. Anthony, Lucretia Mott, and Matilda Joslyn Gage organized the National Woman Suffrage Association, which called itself the National. This group supported sweeping women's rights reforms, including equal pay, marriage reform, equal opportunities for education and employment, equal treatment before the law, divorce reform, and, of course, the right to vote. The National believed that a constitutional amendment was the best way to win suffrage. Because Stanton and Anthony distrusted male reformers after they neglected to include women in the Fourteenth Amendment, the National prohibited men from becoming members.

In November of that same year, Lucy Stone, her husband Henry Blackwell, and Julia Ward Howe organized the American Woman Suffrage Association, which was also called the American Association. Stone's group believed that once women could vote all other social problems for women would be corrected. The American Association also believed that individual states could grant women the right to vote.

The American Association accepted men as members. In order to appear more respectable than Stanton's group, the American Association elected the Reverend Henry Ward Beecher as their president. Beecher was one of the most popular ministers of the nineteenth century and the brother of both the novelist Harriet Beecher Stowe and the women's rights activist Isabella Beecher Hooker. Beecher was famous for his delivery of dramatic antislavery sermons. People traveled from afar to hear him preach in his church in Brooklyn, New York.

Elizabeth Cady Stanton had come to believe that state and national legislatures would never be convinced to change the laws until public attitudes about a woman's role in society changed. Stanton had been disheartened when the Kansas legislature defeated a referendum to give women and African Americans the franchise for the right to vote in November 1867. Kansas was the first state to vote on such a referendum.

Stanton decided to take her message directly to the public. As her children were grown she was free to launch a career as a public speaker at lyceums. In modern usage a lyceum is a hall for public lectures and discussions. In the 1800s, however, the word also meant the lectures themselves.

By the 1870s, at the height of the lyceums' popularity, businesses called lyceum bureaus were established to hire speakers, find jobs for them, advertise events, and negotiate speakers' fees. Improvements to train travel and guaranteed payment made people more willing to work as public speakers. Speakers earned between $100 and $200 for each presentation. The speaker paid for his or her lodging and sent 10 percent of his or her earnings to the lyceum bureau. Although the schedule and the travel were tiring, a speaker could earn a great deal of money. Elizabeth Cady Stanton reported that she earned $2,000 in three months, a sum that at the time was more than many people's annual income.

Most speakers were famous. Popular writers read from their works, including Harriet Beecher Stowe, the author of the best-selling novel *Uncle Tom's Cabin*, and the author and abolitionist Frederick Douglass. Sometimes only the topic was well known, as when reformers talked about temperance or women's rights. By becoming a lyceum speaker and traveling across the country "stirring up women . . . to rebellion,"

OPERA HOUSE, MASSILLON.

ELIZABETH CADY STANTON.

Saturday Evening, Feb'y 6, 1875.

LECTURE, "OUR GIRLS."

This poster advertised a February 6, 1875, lecture that Stanton gave at the Opera House in Massillon, Ohio. In her autobiography Stanton said of her lyceum tours, "The pleasant feature of these trips was the great educational work accomplished for the people through their listening to lectures on all the vital questions of the hour."

Stanton became self-supporting and a celebrity to American women.

From 1869 through 1879, Stanton traveled for eight months each year. She was then in her midfifties and early sixties. Stanton began touring in the fall but returned to New Jersey in December to spend Christmas with her children. She rarely saw her husband Henry. In January she set off again and continued on the lecture circuit until May.

Stanton was an excellent public speaker with a pleasant voice and a gracious manner. Newspapers described her as "plump as a partridge" with white fluffy hair. She

WASHINGTON, D. C.—THE JUDICIARY COMMITTEE OF THE HOUSE OF REPRESENTATIVES RECEIVING A DEPUTATION OF FEMALE SUFFRAGISTS, JANUARY 11TH—A LADY DELEGATE READING HER ARGUMENT IN FAVOR OF WOMAN'S VOTING, ON THE BASIS OF THE FOURTEENTH AND FIFTEENTH CONSTITUTIONAL AMENDMENTS.—SEE PAGE 247.

This engraving of Victoria Woodhull testifying before the House Judiciary Committee on January 11, 1871, on behalf of women's suffrage, appeared in *Frank Leslie's Illustrated Newspaper* on February 4, 1871. Woodhull, an entrepreneur, opened a stock brokerage firm and published a magazine. She ran for the U.S. presidency in 1872.

knew that looking like a grandmother made her words less threatening to her audience, which made them more likely to listen to her. Stanton developed a variety of prepared lectures. Her selection of topics included suffrage, managing the home, raising children, divorce reform, coeducation, and equality in the relationships between men and women.

In 1871, the women's movement gained another voice when the reformer Victoria Woodhull argued before the House Judiciary Committee that women already had the right to vote under the Fourteenth Amendment, which stated that all "persons born or naturalized in the United States" were citizens and protected by the Constitution. If Congress agreed that women in America were persons and that all persons were citizens, then women must be permitted to vote.

Victoria Woodhull was not the first person to use this argument. Virginia Minor, president of the Missouri Woman Suffrage Association, first suggested women had the right to suffrage under the Fourteenth Amendment in 1869. Elizabeth Cady Stanton had published Minor's interpretation in an 1870 issue of the *Revolution* and had used this logic in one of her own speeches. Woodhull was, however, the first person to testify about women's rights before Congress. A special additional hearing was scheduled by Congress to consider the case.

The National was surprised by Woodhull's dramatic appearance in Congress and delighted that a second

The masthead of this April 23, 1868 edition of Stanton and Anthony's weekly suffragist journal, the *Revolution*, displays the publication's motto: "Principle, Not Policy: Justice, Not Favors.—Men, Their Rights And Nothing More: Women, Their Rights And Nothing Less."

hearing was planned. Perhaps another amendment was unnecessary and the vote could be obtained by interpreting existing laws differently.

The National urged women to go to the polls for the next election. Hundreds of women tried to vote in the 1872 presidential election, most notably Virginia Minor of St. Louis, Missouri, and Susan B. Anthony of Rochester, New York.

Almost fifty Rochester women registered to vote in 1872. Sixteen, including Anthony, succeeded in casting their ballots on Election Day. Two weeks later they were arrested and fined for illegal voting. Although some of the women paid their fine, Anthony refused. She wanted a trial. Anthony wanted the Supreme

This June 1873 cartoon made fun of Susan B. Anthony for daring to vote. Gender roles for men and women were rigid in the 1800s. Anthony challenged tradition, so the artist Thomas Wust depicted her in a mannish top hat to resemble Uncle Sam. Wust also mockingly included a woman dressed as a police officer and a man holding a baby.

Court to decide if the Fourteenth Amendment granted women the right to vote as citizens.

Anthony's trial was held in Canandaigua, New York, in June 1873. Judge Ward Hunt refused to let Anthony speak to the jury, declared her guilty, and ordered her to either pay the fine or to go to jail. Anthony refused to pay, saying, " . . . not a penny shall go to this unjust claim." When Anthony's lawyer paid the fine without her knowledge, Anthony's hopes of appealing to the Supreme Court were ended.

Although Anthony's case received more publicity, Virginia Minor's case was actually more significant. Minor had been prevented from voting in Missouri and later sued the registrar of voters, Reese Happersett, for denying Minor her constitutional rights. In 1874, the case of *Minor v. Happersett* reached the Supreme Court. When the Supreme Court ruled in 1875 that national citizenship did not guarantee voting rights, the case proved to reformers that a women's suffrage amendment was needed to obtain the franchise.

By 1879, Elizabeth Cady Stanton was nearly sixty-four years old and the long lyceum schedule had become exhausting. A carriage accident that summer left Stanton bruised and aching. Later that autumn she caught pneumonia. Stanton was ready to return to her home in New Jersey.

7. The History of Women's Rights

On November 12, 1880, Elizabeth Cady Stanton turned sixty-five. Her children had all become adults. Daniel Stanton, her oldest son, had gone to the South after the Civil War and then later returned to the North with a substantial sum of money he had made in Louisiana. The other sons, Henry Jr., Gerrit, Theodore, and Robert, had become lawyers. Theodore was also a journalist and a women's rights reformer. Daughter Margaret went to Vassar College, married, and occasionally worked on behalf of suffrage in New York State. The Stantons' youngest daughter, Harriot, also graduated from Vassar. She married an Englishman in 1882 and became a suffragist in both Great Britain and the United States.

Resigning from the lyceum circuit and returning to live in Tenafly, New Jersey, did not mean that Stanton had retired. Susan B. Anthony kept asking her to write new speeches, which Stanton usually wrote, but documenting the history of women's rights became her priority. The book was a project that Stanton had first considered writing in 1848. Lucretia Mott thought the project was an excellent idea and over the years she pressed Stanton to begin it.

Mott's death shortly after Stanton's sixty-fifth birthday spurred Stanton to document both her friend's and her own work for future generations. She began keeping a personal diary and made plans to write *The History of Woman Suffrage* with Susan B. Anthony and Matilda Gage, another cofounder of the National Woman Suffrage Association. The three women gathered in Tenafly, but Gage soon left New Jersey to care for her sick husband. Anthony disliked all the research and writing necessary for the massive project, but Stanton loved it. Volume I, published in 1881, discussed events from the 1700s until 1860. Volume II covered the history from 1861 to 1876 and was published in May 1882. Volume III brought the history up to 1885 and was published in 1886.

Harriot Stanton, photographed around 1875, was influenced by her mother. Harriot formed a women's rights group and endorsed large protests such as parades and picketing to increase the public's awareness of the suffrage movement.

In May 1882, Stanton's daughter Harriot took her to Europe for a vacation. This was Stanton's first European trip since the 1840 World Anti-Slavery Convention. When Harriot married later that same year, it offered Stanton an excuse to extend her stay in England. She lectured on suffrage, visited with Susan B. Anthony, who was on her own European vacation, and waited for Harriot to have her first child. Nora Stanton Blatch was Stanton's second grandchild. Stanton and Anthony returned to the United States together in November 1883.

Stanton's seventieth birthday in 1885 was celebrated nationally. The National Woman Suffrage Association organized small meetings across the country on November 12. In Manhattan, New York, Stanton read her essay "The Pleasures of Age." Birthday greetings and gifts piled up at her home. "If I were not kept humble by . . . the opposition . . . I am really afraid this . . . might fill me with conceit," she confessed to the editor of the *New Era* when the November issue of the magazine was dedicated to her.

Stanton returned to England in October 1886. In January 1887, she learned that Henry Stanton had died. Although they had been unofficially separated for fifteen years, Elizabeth and Henry had remained caring friends. The news of his death saddened her. "If we could only remember in life to be gentle and [patient] with each other," she admitted in her diary, "our memories of the past would be more pleasant." Stanton missed Henry more than she had expected to, but widowhood was not as difficult for her as it was for many women at the time.

Stanton owned her own house, had her own money, and would not be forced to give up her home.

The year 1888 marked the fortieth anniversary of the Seneca Falls Convention. In commemoration, or to honor and remember the event, Anthony organized the International Council of Women in March and invited the original Seneca Falls supporters to attend. Anthony also hoped to reunite the two parts of the women's movement. Stanton was still living in England at the time. Stanton looked forward to the meeting, but crossing the Atlantic Ocean in the winter when the water was rough and choppy was not something she wanted to do.

After Anthony warned Stanton that she would never forgive her if she did not come, Stanton agreed to make the trip. Delayed by the worst blizzard of the nineteenth century, Stanton finally arrived in Washington, D.C., only days before the council. She had not prepared a speech. As the story goes, Anthony locked Stanton in a guarded hotel room until Stanton appeared three days later with what Anthony called a "magnificent address."

While in Washington, Stanton testified before the Senate on behalf of suffrage. Speaking before a legislature no longer intimidated Stanton, and she felt smarter than most of the senators. Stanton also noticed that she and Anthony were beginning to think differently, too. "I get more radical as I get older while Susan seems to grow more conservative," Stanton confided to her diary.

This is an 1888 photograph of the first International Council of Women, which met in Washington, D.C. By inviting international delegates, Anthony (*first row, second from left*) and Stanton (*first row, fourth from left*) hoped to expand the women's rights movement and create a bond of "universal sisterhood." More than fifty-three national women's groups participated in the event as well.

The women's movement merger Anthony had hoped for finally occurred in February 1890, when the National American Woman Suffrage Association (NAWSA), was formed. Stanton was elected president and Anthony was elected vice president. Conservative members of NAWSA led by Lucy Stone were worried that Stanton would make the group too radical. Stanton, however, was no longer interested in attending conventions. She accepted the presidency and departed for her daughter Harriot's house in England.

Relieved, the conservatives wished her a happy trip and asked Anthony to lead the meetings in her absence.

In January 1891, Stanton received the crushing news that her son Daniel was dead. He was her only child to die before she did. Four months later Stanton's oldest sister, Tryphena, died. Stanton returned to the United States. Anthony invited her to share her home in Rochester, but Stanton was afraid she would be kept busy writing speeches all the time and declined the offer. Instead Stanton sold the house in Tenafly and purchased an apartment in Manhattan with her son and daughter.

Stanton reluctantly agreed to give a speech at the 1892 NAWSA meeting in Washington, D.C. Stanton had spent time thinking about her life and its tragedies, and in the speech her words reflected this meditation. Unlike her usual inspiring speeches, "The Solitude of Self" was somber. Stanton reminded listeners of "the individuality of each human soul." Everyone is born alone, suffers alone, and dies alone. Therefore, every man and woman must be equally trained to be self-reliant. Most people thought this was Stanton's best speech. Anthony, however, disliked it. Stanton read the speech to Congress before returning home.

Stanton had been a plump little girl, and she contin-ued to gain weight as she aged. By her late seventies, she weighed so much that she could hardly move. Her intelligence was as sharp as ever and she continued to publish articles in a wide range of newspapers and magazines. When Stanton turned eighty in 1895, Anthony quietly coordinated NAWSA's celebration. Banners and flowers filled the Metropolitan Opera House. Three hours of praise from both friends and former foes filled the evening. Stanton was touched. She was too weak to read her speech because of her weight, but she rose to thank the audience: "I am well aware that these demonstrations are not so much tributes to me . . . as to the great idea that I represent—the enfranchisement of women." She received a standing ovation. Only a few weeks later, Stanton and a number of cowriters published her most controversial work, *The Woman's Bible*.

Elizabeth Cady Stanton's eightieth birthday celebration was held on November 12, 1895, at the Metropolitan Opera House in New York City. One fan wrote to Stanton that every "woman owes her liberty largely to yourself and to your earliest and bravest co-workers."

The Woman's Bible
— Chapter II —
by
Elizabeth Cady Stanton

(long small) Genesis II 21 – 25.
print

21 And the LORD God caused a deep sleep
to fall upon Adam, and he slept; and he
took one of his ribs, and closed up the flesh
instead thereof.
22 And the rib, which the LORD God had
taken from man, made he a woman, and
brought her unto the man.
23 And Adam said, This is now bone of my
bones, and flesh of my flesh: she shall be
called Woman, because she was taken out
of man.
24 Therefore shall a man leave his father
and his mother, and shall cleave unto his
wife: and they shall be one flesh.
25 And they were both naked, the man and
his wife, and were not ashamed.

As the account of the creation in the first chapter, is in harmony with science, common sense & the experience of mankind in natural laws, the enquiry naturally arises why should there be two contradictory accounts in the same book, of the same event? It is fair to infer that the second version, which is found in some form, in the different religions of all nations, is a mere allegory, symbolizing some mysterious conception of a

___

This is a manuscript page from Chapter II of *The Woman's Bible*.
Stanton pasted clippings from the Bible's book of Genesis in the center
of the page. This was either to guide her thoughts as she wrote or a
reference to the printer of passages she wanted to include in the book.

The project was conceived in 1881, after another book called the *New Revised Bible* was released. This work made it seem that biblical study and reinterpretation was acceptable. Stanton, who read Greek and Latin and studied philosophy and religion, asked several female scholars to help her study the Bible from a woman's point of view. Five women agreed to help. They were the Reverend Phebe Hanaford, Ellen B. Dietrich, Ursula Gestafield, Louisa Southworth, and Frances E. Burr. Anthony tried in vain to stop Stanton from undertaking this project, saying it would only create additional enemies for the women's movement.

Stanton had long been dismayed at how ministers and religious groups interpreted the Bible. Their interpretations were used to justify the treatment of women as second-class citizens and to endorse the domination of women by men. Stanton pointed out that although ministers frequently quoted a biblical passage in the Book of Genesis that says Eve was created from the rib of Adam, there is another passage in Genesis that says both women and men were created at the same time, in the image of God.

Although many of Stanton's comments and interpretations of the Bible have become widely accepted by churches today, at the time, her sarcastic tone embarrassed her religious friends and made the general public call her a heretic. Stanton did not care. She had men and women thinking and debating. The book

This is a photograph of Elizabeth Cady Stanton's desk in her apartment in New York City's Upper West Side. When Stanton moved to the city around 1892, her life in a one-floor apartment took some getting used to. Stanton said that she "had always lived in a large house."

was a best seller and was eventually translated into several languages.

Conservative women in the NAWSA were disturbed by the book. They voted to censure, or officially disagree with, *The Woman's Bible*. Anthony reminded the delegates that Lucretia Mott had once thought asking for the vote too radical, and that many people in the 1860s thought that making drunkenness grounds for divorce was also too radical. Perhaps people would someday think *The Woman's Bible* was not too radical either. Besides, Anthony continued, men interpreted the Bible all the time. The NAWSA conservatives did not accept Anthony's defense of Stanton and hoped Stanton would resign. Not only did Stanton remain president of NAWSA, but also she printed their letter of disapproval in later editions of *The Woman's Bible*.

8. The Battle Must Finish with Another Generation

In 1898, Elizabeth Cady Stanton published her autobiography, *Eighty Years and More.* The book skipped over many of the difficult passages of Stanton's life, including her disagreements with her husband Henry and Daniel Cady's anger over his daughter's work toward reform.

Susan B. Anthony visited Stanton in Manhattan in June 1902, and planned to return for Stanton's birthday in November. Anthony wrote to Stanton in 1902:

I shall indeed be happy to spend with you November 12. . . . It is fifty-one years since first we met and we have been busy through every one of them, stirring up the world to recognize the rights of women. . . . We little dreamed when we began this contest . . . that half a century later we would be compelled to leave the finish of the battle to another generation of women. But our hearts are filled with joy to know that they . . . [have] a college education, . . . business experience, [and] . . . the fully admitted right to speak in public, — all of

*which were denied to women fifty years ago. . . .
And we dear old friend, shall move on to the next
sphere of existence . . . where women will not be
placed in an inferior position but will be wel-
comed on a plane of perfect intellectual and spiritual equality.*

Elizabeth Cady Stanton died on October 26, 1902, less
than two weeks before her eighty-seventh birthday. In
spite of being blind, overweight, and continuously short
of breath, Stanton had continued to lobby for women's

Alongside the flower-laden casket of Elizabeth Cady Stanton is a
picture of Susan B. Anthony. Stanton was later buried in Woodlawn
Cemetery in Bronx, New York.

suffrage. Only days before her death from heart failure, she sent President Theodore Roosevelt a letter urging him to support the women's suffrage amendment. On the day Stanton died, she asked her nurse to help her out of bed. Leaning her hands on a table, she stood silently for several minutes. Her daughter Harriot believed that she was giving a silent speech. Then, apparently pleased with herself, she returned to her armchair and fell asleep. Stanton died without waking a few hours later.

Stanton's death was on the front page of many newspapers around the world. The press called her "America's Grand Old Woman." Hundreds of people

Above: After Stanton's death the fight for women's rights continued. About 20,000 suffragists marched down Fifth Avenue in New York City on May 6, 1912, on behalf of women's rights. To show their solidarity, or unity toward a shared goal or cause, the women all dressed in white.

sent sympathy notes to the family. The 1903 NAWSA meeting included a memorial service. Reporters knocked on Susan B. Anthony's door in Rochester seeking a comment from her. "If I had died first she would have found beautiful phrases to describe our friendship, but I cannot put it into words," Anthony replied. Six months later Anthony confided to Stanton's son Theodore, "How lonesome I do feel. . . . It was a great going out of my life when she went."

Stanton left instructions for her funeral. "I should like to be in my ordinary dress . . . and some common sense women to conduct the services." Reverend Phebe Hanaford, a coauthor of *The Woman's Bible*, presided over the burial. At the head of the coffin was the table where Stanton had written the Declaration of Rights and

Sentiments. On top of the table lay a copy of *The History of Woman Suffrage*. A portrait of Susan B. Anthony was placed alongside Stanton's flower-laden casket.

Susan B. Anthony carried on the work for suffrage for another three and one-half years. Working with Ida Husted Harper, Anthony wrote Volume IV of *The History of Woman Suffrage*. On February 15, 1906, a large birthday party was held for Anthony in Washington, D.C. Later that evening Anthony made a speech and concluded by saying that with all the great women who had dedicated their lives to obtaining suffrage for women, "Failure is impossible!"

When Susan B. Anthony died on March 13, 1906, she was eighty-six years old. Days before her death she had confided to a friend, "Just think, I have been striving for over sixty years for a little bit of justice . . . and yet I must die without obtaining it. . . . It seems so cruel."

•　•　•　•

In 1919, Congress finally passed the Nineteenth Amendment to the U.S. Constitution, which gave women the vote. However, thirty-six states had to agree in order for the amendment to become law. On a steamy August

Previous Spread: Harriot Stanton Blatch, daughter of Elizabeth Cady Stanton, was photographed around 1915 as she spoke before a crowd of men on New York City's Wall Street. Blatch was "stump speaking" on behalf of women's rights. Stump speaking is a political expression. It means to promote a cause or to publicize the election of a candidate to a political office by going from town to town to campaign before the people.

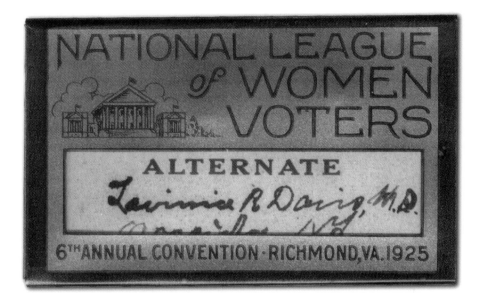

This badge was worn by a member of the National League of Women Voters in 1925 at the organization's sixth annual convention. Members of the National American Woman Suffrage Association began organizing the group in 1919. After voting rights for women were secured, the league sought to prevent discrimination against women and to encourage women to register to vote.

day in 1920, the Tennessee legislature considered the women's suffrage amendment. If Tennessee approved the amendment, women in the United States would be allowed to cast their ballot on Election Day.

Suffragists lobbied hard. They presented signed petitions in favor of the amendment and met with legislators to persuade them to approve it. Still, the count was too close to be certain of the outcome. One by one, the names of the Tennessee legislators were called, and man by man they answered yes or no. Twenty-four-year-old Harry Burn cast the deciding vote.

This 1920 photograph, taken at the National Woman's Party headquarters in Washington, D.C., shows the suffragist Alice Paul holding a victory flag that is decorated with stars. Each star symbolized a state that had ratified the Nineteenth Amendment to the U.S. Constitution.

Harry Burn wore an antisuffrage red rose on his suit jacket, but carried a note from his mother in his pocket. When his name was called, he voted yes, just as his mother had asked him to do. Seventy-two years after Elizabeth Cady Stanton had stood in Seneca Falls and timidly asked for the right to vote, the battle was over.

Timeline

1815	Elizabeth Cady is born on November 12 in Johnstown, New York.
1833	Elizabeth Cady graduates from Troy Female Seminary.
1840	Elizabeth Cady and Henry B. Stanton marry on May 1 in Johnstown, NY. The newlyweds travel to London to attend the World Anti-Slavery Convention.
1843–45	Stanton helps collect signatures and lobbies the New York legislature to pass the Married Woman's Property Act. The act passes in New York in 1848.
1848	On July 19 and 20, the Seneca Falls Woman's Rights Convention is held.
1850	On October 23, the first National Woman's Rights Convention is held in Worcester, Massachusetts. Stanton sends a letter outlining the agenda.
1851	Elizabeth Cady Stanton meets Susan B. Anthony in May.
1854	Stanton testifies on women's rights on February 14, in front of the New York State legislature.
1861	On April 12, Fort Sumter is attacked and the Civil War begins.
1862	Henry Stanton receives a job as deputy collector of customs for the Port Authority of New York. The Stantons move to New York City.
1863	On January 1, the Emancipation Proclamation frees African Americans in the rebelling states. In March, Stanton and Anthony form the National Woman's Loyal League to gain support for the Thirteenth Amendment.
1865	On April 9, Confederate general Robert E. Lee

surrenders to Union general Ulysses S. Grant, ending the Civil War. In June, the Thirteenth Amendment is ratified and slavery is outlawed across the United States. Stanton and Anthony petition the U.S. Congress for women's suffrage for the first time.

1866   Stanton and Anthony form the American Equal Rights Association. Stanton runs for U.S. Congress in New York. She receives twenty-four votes.

1867   Stanton appears before the suffrage subcommittee of the New York Constitutional Convention in June demanding that suffrage be extended to all property-owning, taxpaying adults regardless of race or gender.

1868   Stanton and Anthony begin publishing the *Revolution* in January. In July the Fourteenth Amendment is ratified, granting suffrage to "Negro males."

1869   The National Woman Suffrage Association is formed on May 11 with Stanton as president. The American Woman Suffrage Association is formed that same year with Lucy Stone as president.

1875   The Supreme Court rules in *Minor v. Happersett* that women are not constitutionally entitled to vote.

1878   A Constitutional amendment for women's suffrage is introduced in Congress. The Senate votes against the measure. The amendment is introduced every year until it is finally passed in 1919.

1879   Stanton retires from lyceum tours.

1881   Volume I of *The History of Woman Suffrage* is published. Volumes II and III are published in 1882 and 1886 respectively.

1882   Stanton travels to England.

1902   Elizabeth Cady Stanton dies on October 26.

Glossary

abstained (ab-STAYND) To have chosen not to do something.

adjournment (uh-JERN-ment) To bring a meeting to an end, temporarily.

advocate (AD-vuh-kayt) To speak in favor of.

boisterous (BOY-stres) High-spirited; very energetic.

bustle (BUH-sul) To be filled with energy and activity.

civil rights (SIH-vul RYTS) The rights that citizens have.

convened (kun-VEEND) To have assembled together as a group.

cordial (KOR-jel) Warm or cheerful.

custody (KUS-tuh-dee) To direct the care of and have control over someone, especially a child.

delegate (DEH-lih-get) A representative elected to attend a political gathering.

effigy (EH-fuh-jee) A crude figure or dummy that represents a hated person.

entrepreneur (on-truh-pruh-NUR) A businessperson who has started his or her own business.

equate (ih-KWAYT) To draw a connection between two different concepts or things and consider them to be equal.

feminists (FEH-mih-nists) People who believe that women should have social and legal rights equal to those of men.

franchise (FRAN-chyz) A right or privilege that is granted to a person or to a group.

gender (JEN-der) Relating to a person's sex, male or female.

heathen (HEE-then) A person who does not practice or accept the religion of the people who are trying to convert that person.

heretic (HER-uh-tik) Someone whose opinions, especially with regard to religion, differ from what is generally accepted.

Hicksite Quakers (HIK-syt KWAY-kurz) People who belonged to a radical branch of Quakerism, named for Elias Hicks. They believed that men and women had equal spiritual gifts and deserved an equal right and obligation to speak out against wrongdoing. All Quakers, including the Hicksites, believed everyone, regardless of gender or race, was equal before God and should be equal before the law.

immorality (ih-moh-RA-lih-tee) The quality of being outside of what society considers to be normal and acceptable behavior.

inalienable (ih-NAYL-yeh-nuh-bul) Something that cannot be surrendered.

indecent (in-DEE-sent) Something that is considered to be improper or rude.

inseparable (in-SEH-puh-ruh-bul) United and difficult to separate.

intimidated (in-TIH-muh-dayt-ed) To have made someone timid or afraid.

militia (muh-LIH-shuh) A group of volunteer or citizen soldiers who are organized to assemble in emergencies.

mortifying (MOR-tuh-fy-ing) Describing an experience that causes a feeling of shame or discomfort.

orthodox (OR-thuh-doks) To be conservative or to observe a traditional way of thinking.

outraged (OWT-rayjd) Extremely angry.

pacifist (PA-suh-fist) Someone who opposes the use of force, especially military action, under any circumstances.

pauper (PAH-per) A person who is extremely poor.

preside (prih-ZYD) To lead or to be in a position of authority.

prohibited (PROH-hih-bih-ted) To have forbidden someone from doing something.

radicals (RA-dih-kulz) People who have ideas that are not widely accepted and who express these ideas in ways meant to get attention.

referendum (reh-feh-REN-dem) The practice of submitting a question to the public on a proposed change or addition to legislative policy to have the public vote on it.

registrar (REH-jih-strahr) A person in charge of official records.

revivals (rih-VY-vulz) Passionate religious services.

scourging (SKERJ-ing) Punishing with a whip or with words.

seceded (sih-SEED-ed) Withdrew from a group or a country.

servitude (SER-vih-tood) A condition in which an individual lacks the freedom to choose a course of action for herself or himself.

shanties (SHAN-teez) Roughly built huts or shacks.

sobriety (suh-BRY-eh-tee) The quality of being serious, calm, or earnest.

spheres (SFEERZ) Areas of activity or interest that are associated with a particular person or group.

stock brokerage firm (STOK BROH-keh-rij FERM) A business in which men or women buy or sell investments in other companies for their customers.

suffrage (SUH-frij) The right of voting.

temperance (TEM-puh-rents) Originally the belief that drinking alcohol should be tempered, or consumed in moderate doses and limited to wine, beer, and cider. Later temperance came to mean not drinking any alcohol at all. Since no laws protected wives or children from abuse by drunken husbands or fathers, reformers sought to make drinking illegal.

thrived (THRYVD) To have been successful; to have done well.

unmolested (un-muh-LEST-ed) Remaining peaceful and avoiding becoming annoyed.

U.S. Constitution (YOO ES kon-stih-TOO-shun) The document adopted in 1788 that explains the different parts of the nation's government and how each part works.

vengeance (VEN-jens) Punishment for an injury or an offense.

Additional Resources

If you would like to learn more about Elizabeth Cady Stanton and women's suffrage, check out the following books and Web sites:

Books

Adams, Colleen. *Women's Suffrage: A Primary Source History of the Women's Rights Movement in America*. New York: The Rosen Publishing Group, 2003.

Faber, Doris. *Oh Lizzie: The Life of Elizabeth Cady Stanton*. New York: Lothrop, Lee & Shepard, 1972.

Web Sites

Due to the changing nature of Internet links, PowerPlus Books has developed an online list of Web sites related to the subject of this book. This site is updated regularly. Please use this link to access the list:
www.powerkidslinks.com/lalt/ecstanton/

Bibliography

Banner, Lois W. *Elizabeth Cady Stanton: A Radical for Women's Rights.* Boston: Little, Brown, 1980.

Blackwell, Alice Stone. *Lucy Stone: Pioneer of Woman's Rights.* Charlottesville, VA: University Press of Virginia, 2001.

Conrad, Susan P. *Perish the Thought: Intellectual Women in Romantic America, 1830–1860.* New York: Oxford University Press, 1978.

Dubois, Ellen Carol, ed. *The Elizabeth Cady Stanton–Susan B. Anthony Reader: Correspondence, Writings, Speeches.* Rev. ed. Boston: Northeastern University Press, 1992.

Flexner, Eleanor. *Century of Struggle.* New York: Atheneum, 1973.

Gordon, Ann D., ed. *The Selected Papers of Elizabeth Cady Stanton and Susan B. Anthony.* Vol. 1. New Brunswick, NJ: Rutgers University Press, 1997.

Griffith, Elisabeth, *In Her Own Right: The Life of Elizabeth Cady Stanton.* New York: Oxford University Press, 1984.

Hewitt, Nancy A. *Women's Activism and Social Change: Rochester, New York, 1822–1872.* Ithaca, NY: Cornell University Press, 1984.

Larkin, Jack. *The Reshaping of Everyday Life., 1790–1840.* New York: Harper Perennial & Row, 1989.

Sigerman, Harriet. *Elizabeth Cady Stanton: The Right is Ours.* New York: Oxford University Press, 2001.

Stanton, Elizabeth Cady. *Eighty Years and More 1815–1897: Reminiscences of Elizabeth Cady Stanton.* New York: European Publishing Co., 1898.

Stanton, Henry B. *Random Recollections.* New York: Harper & Bros, 1887.

Stanton, Theodore and Harriot Stanton Blatch, eds. *Elizabeth Cady Stanton as Revealed in Her Letters, Diary and Reminiscences.* Vols. 1 and 2. New York: Harper & Bros., 1922.

Ward, Geoffrey C. *Not For Ourselves Alone: The Story of Elizabeth Cady Stanton and Susan B. Anthony.* New York: Alfred A. Knopf, 1999.

Index

About the Author

Dawn C. Adiletta, curator of the Harriet Beecher Stowe Center in Hartford, Connecticut, is a historian, an author, and a lecturer. She has worked as a consultant for museums and historical societies throughout New England, including Old Sturbridge Village, the Connecticut Antiquaries and Landmarks Society, and the Clara Barton Birthplace. Adiletta has written about New England quilt makers, historic houses, and women's history. Ms. Adiletta sits on the board of the National Collaborative of Women's History sites, a network designed to promote and teach women's history throughout the United States. She lives in Woodstock, Connecticut, with her husband.

Primary Sources

Cover: Elizabeth Cady Stanton, photograph, circa 1870s, Napoleon Sarony, courtesy of Coline Jenkins, the Elizabeth Cady Stanton Trust. Background, Convention for Women's Suffrage hosted by the National Woman's Suffrage Association, 1880. **Page 4.** Elizabeth Cady Stanton, oil painting, Anna Elizabeth Klumpke, 1889, National Portrait Gallery, Smithsonian Institution. **Page 8.** The Cady home in Johnstown, New York, photograph, circa mid-1900s, courtesy of Coline Jenkins, the Elizabeth Cady Stanton Trust. **Page 11.** Daniel Cady, oil painting, 1800s, courtesy of Coline Jenkins, the Elizabeth Cady Stanton Trust. **Page 12.** Margaret Livingston Cady, oil painting, circa 1840, Women's Rights National Historical Park, National Park Service. **Page 15.** *The Polymircrian Greek Lexicon to the New Testament*, book, 1829, written by William Greenfield, courtesy of Coline Jenkins, the Elizabeth Cady Stanton Trust. **Page 16.** Advertisement for the Troy Female Seminary, engraving, mid-1800s, Emma Willard School Archives. **Page 17.** *Camp Meeting*, lithograph, circa 1829, Hugh Bridport, based on a work by Alexander Rider, Library of Congress Prints and Photographs Division. **Page 19.** Gerrit Smith, daguerreotype, circa 1850, Ezra Greenleaf Weld, National Portrait Gallery, Smithsonian Institution. **Page 21.** *Declaration of the Anti-Slavery Convention*, broadside, December 4, 1833, Reuben S. Gilbert, Library of Congress Rare Book and Special Collections Division. **Page 22.** Dr. Edward Bayard, photograph, 1800s, courtesy of Coline Jenkins, Elizabeth Cady Stanton Trust. **Page 24.** *The Anti-Slavery Society Convention, 1841*, oil painting, 1841, Benjamin Robert Haydon, National Portrait Gallery, London. **Page 25.** Lucretia Coffin Mott, oil painting, 1842, Joseph Kyle, National Portrait Gallery, Smithsonian Institution. **Page 27.** Elizabeth Cady Stanton with her son Henry Jr., photograph, circa 1854, courtesy of Coline Jenkins, the Elizabeth Cady Stanton Trust. **Page 29.** Seneca Falls, New York, daguerreotype, circa 1855, Smithsonian American Art Museum. **Page 31.** *Ye May session of ye woman's rights convention. Ye orator of ye day denouncing ye lords of creation*, engraving, 1859, Library of Congress, Prints and Photograph Division. **Page 32.** "Declaration of Rights and Sentiments," 1848, printed in the July 14, 1848 *Seneca County Courier*, National American Woman Suffrage Association Collection, Library of Congress. **Page 35.** Elizabeth Cady Stanton speaking at the Seneca Falls Convention, illustration, circa 1869. **Page 36.** Our Roll of Honor, copy of the original signers of the "Declaration of Rights and Sentiments," 1908, Library of Congress Manuscript Division. **Page 38.** *The Lily*, February 1, 1855, courtesy of Coline Jenkins, the Elizabeth Cady Stanton Trust. **Page 39.** *The bloomer costume*, lithograph, 1851, Currier & Ives, Library of Congress. **Page 43.** Susan B. Anthony, photograph, circa 1870, Napoleon Sarony, State Historical Society of Wisconsin Visual Archives. **Page 45.** Letter from Elizabeth Cady Stanton to Susan B. Anthony, March 1, 1852, Library of Congress, Manuscript Division. **Page 46.** *The Confirmed Drunkard*, one of four scenes from *The Drunkard's*

Progress, or the Direct Route to Poverty, Wretchedness & Ruin, engraving, circa 1826, John Warner Barber, Library of Congress Prints and Photographs Division. **Page 48.** "Address to the Legislature of New York," which was adopted by the State Woman's Rights Convention, 1854, Elizabeth Cady Stanton, published by Parsons Weed, courtesy of Coline Jenkins, the Elizabeth Cady Stanton Trust.. **Page 51.** Elizabeth Cady Stanton and Susan B. Anthony, photograph, circa 1870, Napoleon Sarony, National Portrait Gallery, Smithsonian Institution. **Page 52.** Albany, N.Y., drawn from nature, watercolor, 1845, Augustus B. Köllner, Phelps Stokes Collection, Miriam and Ira D. Wallach Division of Art, Prints, and Photographs, the New York Public Library, Astor, Lenox, and Tilden Foundations. **Page 55.** Lucy Stone, photograph, circa 1850, Library of Congress Prints and Photographs Division. **Page 56.** Henry B. Stanton, photograph, courtesy of Coline Jenkins, the Elizabeth Cady Stanton Trust. **Pages 58–59.** *Rioters sacking the Brownstone Houses in New York*, engraving, 1863, Library of Congress Prints and Photographs Division. **Page 61.** *Through the weary years of the war Clara Barton stayed at her post*, engraving, early 1900s, William Merie Allison, Library of Congress Prints and Photographs Division. **Page 64.** The House Joint Resolution proposing the 13th amendment to the Constitution, 1861, National Archives and Records Administration. **Page 67.** *The First Vote*, engraving, 1867, Alfred R. Waud, Library of Congress Prints and Photograph Division. **Page 68.** Clipping announcing Elizabeth Cady Stanton running for the U.S. Congress from New York State, October 13, 1866, *National Anti-Slavery Standard*. **Page 70.** Stanton's home in Tenafly, New Jersey, modern photograph by Mr. Jeffrey Wendt. **Page 73.** Poster advertising one of Stanton's lyceum tours, lithograph, 1875, W. Dreser, Massillon Museum, Ohio. **Page 74.** Victoria Woodhull, engraving, published in Frank Leslie's Illustrated Newspaper, February 4, 1871, Library of Congress Prints and Photograph Division. **Page 76.** *The Revolution*, April 23, 1868, first page, courtesy of Coline Jenkins, the Elizabeth Cady Stanton Trust. **Page 77.** *The woman who dared*, engraving, 1873, Thomas Wust. **Page 80.** Harriot Stanton, photograph, circa 1875, courtesy of Coline Jenkins, the Elizabeth Cady Stanton Trust. **Page 83.** First International Council of Women, photograph, 1888, Library of Congress Prints and Photographs Division. **Page 85.** Reception in honor of Mrs. Stanton at the Metropolitan Opera House, New York, photograph, 1895, Special Collections and University Archives, Rutgers University. **Page 86.** *The Woman's Bible*, manuscript page, Elizabeth Cady Stanton, Library of Congress, Manuscript Division. **Page 88.** Interior of Elizabeth Cady Stanton New York City apartment, photograph, courtesy of Coline Jenkins, the Elizabeth Cady Stanton Trust. **Page 91.** Stanton's Casket, covered with flowers, photograph, 1902, Special Collections and University Archives, Rutgers University Libraries. **Pages 92–93.** Suffrage parade, New York City, photograph, May 6, 1912, Library of Congress Prints and Photograph Division. **Page 94–95.** Mrs. Harriot Stanton Blatch speaking to a crowd on Wall Street, photograph, circa 1915, courtesy of Coline Jenkins, the Elizabeth Cady Stanton Trust. **Page 97.** Badge worn by member of the National League of Women Voters, 1925, courtesy of Coline Jenkins, the Elizabeth Cady Stanton Trust. **Page 98.** Alice Paul unfurls a flag representing the states that had ratified the 19th Amendment from the balcony of the National Women's Party headquarters in Washington DC, photograph, 1920, Library of Congress Prints and Photographs Division.

Credits